D1434800

Church of the Isles

Church of the Isles

The Emerging Church in Britain and Ireland –
a prophetic strategy for renewal

Ray Simpson

STUDY GUIDE INCLUDED

kevin mayhew

First published in 2003 by

KEVIN MAYHEW LTD
Buxhall, Stowmarket, Suffolk, IP14 3BW
info@kevinmayhewltd.com
www.kevinmayhew.com

9 8 7 6 5 4 3 2 1

ISBN-10: 1 84417 107 8
ISBN-13: 978 1 84417 107 1
Catalogue No: 1500605

Cover design by Jaquetta Sergeant
Typeset by Carol Palmer

Printed and bound in Great Britain

Contents

Dedication

I dedicate this book to my many friends who are pioneering new ways of being church; and to Ian Bradley and John Finney, two advisors who have helped me in preparing this book, and whose contributions to the emerging church are invaluable.

Ian Bradley's tutoring of young potential leaders, introducing them to the experience of the early churches of the British Isles and to pioneers of mission is reflected in his prophetic book *Colonies of Heaven*. John Finney's books *Understanding Leadership, How People Find Faith,* and *Recovering the Past: Celtic and Roman Models* each help us to understand how to become the People's Church.

I am grateful to John Sumner, leader of Glastonbury's Quest Community, for sharing with me so much of his fresh thinking, born in the crucible of the church on the edges, and for extracts from his writings quoted in this book.

RAY SIMPSON

About the Author

Ray Simpson has been a minister in churches in the industrial Midlands, multi-racial London and rural East Anglia, and he has planted a neighbourhood church in Bowthorpe, Norwich as described in chapter seven. Here he was both a Church of England vicar and a Free Church minister. He has been involved in renewal movements and in the training of church leaders. Since moving to Lindisfarne in 1996 he has been a consultant to pastors and priests who are at the work face of the emerging church, and has networked with congregations who are seeking fresh models. He is the Guardian of the Community of Aidan and Hilda.

Note for Churches outside the British and Irish Isles –

Although this book largely focuses on the emerging Church in the British and Irish Isles, it has an application for the Church in many other lands.

CHAPTER 1

The Dream

I am a visitor returning to the land I last saw back in the second millennium. I decide to explore its high streets. The same pavement advertisements that were fashionable then are still there ('Aromatherapy' here, 'Hypnotism' there) but now intriguing new ones appear alongside them. 'Sister Diane's Listening Hours – book an appointment'; 'Find your calling sessions with Brother Ted'. Brother Ted informed me that nowadays churches use a blend of technology and their own unique insights to offer temperament, aptitude and vocational guidance on most high streets. This wasn't obvious to me at first, for most of the churches are cafés. Next to a small town vegetable market I notice this placard: 'Meditation sessions every weekday at midday and 6pm with the brothers of Watersprings Community Church'.

Technology has transformed every shop and facility I enter; everything seems digitalised. This includes churches, for they have brought to life God's Hand in their history through their digital education areas; but it seems churches are the only places left where people have the space to find their true selves. I met an inner-city fellowship of contemplatives. They kept several churches as places where anyone could paint or pray with icons. 'Churches will soon be the only environments where people are not drugged,' one of them said. 'Many will plug their brains into computer gaming environments all day. Churches will be the only spaces where people can breathe freely, think their own thoughts and be truly free.'

His colleague conversed about the change in people's concept of time. 'Scientists say that the concept of past, present and future is out of date. They speak about an eternal Now. But they don't know how to connect this discovery to ordinary life,' he confided in me. When I queried who *would* know how to, he put a list of church addresses into my hand.

As I visited these, I realised that a phenomenon is taking place. It evidently started with Black Pentecostals, but now it marks both new and old churches. Someone breaks bread and pours out wine during their main celebrations. Bells are rung, or there is a music extravaganza or dancing, or in some churches a pregnant silence. They call it *anamnesis*, meaning that at that same moment everyone is back at the Cross on which Jesus Christ was put to death in the first Christian century, is plugged into the pouring out of Christ's presence now, and is foretasting their celebrations with him in the future. This is exciting and for real; nobody who experiences this needs drugs.

The shopping centre Christian village

I come to a town with a huge indoor shopping complex. It has various 'villages', each with its distinctive style. Sandwiched between the Mediterranean and the Chinese villages is the Christian village. This has shops for whole food, fair trade produce, third world clothes, local crafts and food grown organically on the church's allotments. There is a free crèche facility for shoppers, and a busking area where various local music groups perform. A large open-plan café leads into various rooms. One room has icons and is for anyone who wishes to stay in silence. Another has a fountain and pool. Here anyone can bring their baby, a new acquisition or even an aged relative to be blessed. I observed that the person on duty was dressed in a white two-piece tunic with a large cross hanging around his neck. He had eye contact with those who came and drew out deeper things for which they welcomed prayer. This man used the desk intercom to ring someone in another part of the building. He had evidently booked his visitor in to their counselling service. On another door was this notice: 'Christian Village Enquiries'. I entered and asked for a guide. A stylishly dressed woman in her late forties, with dyed auburn hair, led me up an escalator to a large auditorium. It had a stage, and the latest in spotlights and musical apparatus. 'We hold our worship sessions here in the evenings,' she informed me, 'and on weekdays we have our body-soul aerobics.' The escalator to the third floor led us to six flats. Here the church's full-time staff lived.

'How can you afford all this?' I asked the auburn lady. 'It's like this,' she explained. 'Long ago local rulers gave prime spaces to Christian communities because they knew that, although they had no possessions, they brought blessing to the life and work around them. Today, multi-national companies who own shopping centres have the same idea. They know that people do not live by shopping alone. They give a prime space to a Christian network with a good track record in holistic service, prayer and friendship.'

Although I was deeply impressed with this Christian Village, I feared lest other shopping villages had been left without any spiritual resources. So it was a relief, in a shopping village a hundred miles north, to experience shades of the Call of the Minaret: the screens in each shop flashed 'Prayer' for five minutes before the tills opened and before midday and twilight. I followed the direction of the arrows on the screens. A handful of people were kneeling on prayer stools, dressed in tunics of sackcloth with cantilevered edging. One of them gave each arrival a card containing the worship pattern for the day. There were some singing, reading, plenty of silence, and prayer for local needs. One of the seven read out prayer request slips, which shoppers had put in an illuminated container during the day. At the close of the five minutes the leader invited everyone to leave or to stay in silence for as long they wished. That was all. There were no ancillary projects. No catches. No charges, just a bowl for donations.

I lingered until the last person in cantilevered sackcloth was about to leave, and plied her with questions. 'Who are you? How did this come about? What do you live on?' 'Churches Together put the idea to the local shops, and invited volunteers,' she told me. 'Following appraisal seven of us were commissioned. Two retired early, one is taking a year out before university, two have part-time jobs, and two are living on the donations we receive. We don't come here on Sundays, we go to our own churches and keep Sunday special.'

The downtown Loaves and Fishes church

A dreary drive took me to a seedy town. Groups of junkies huddled in doorways. I loitered in a café until it closed. I shivered as I noticed that shops all along the street were boarded up, until a distant sound of music drew nearer. It was a cavalcade, brightly lit, full of bright-faced people each wearing an apron on which was blazoned loaves and fishes. They invited anyone to come on board and eat broth from a heated urn and delicious-smelling homemade bread.

A hand shook mine and a voice said, 'Hello, I'm Guy, the leader of the Loaves and Fishes; we're one of the projects of the Highway Christian Fellowship.' We got into deep conversation. As dark drew near, Guy asked if I'd like to stay the night with them. 'We live in the neck-end of this town that was gutted after civil riots five years ago. We moved into some redundant buildings. With volunteers from around the country, plus grants and donations, we've transformed this place. Twenty-six of us live there, about two hundred join in our worship on Sundays, and about fifty each evening.'

Guy was quite a thinker. 'You see, the world is divided into two groups, those who can use technology and have money, and those who can't. These become anti-social addicts, often violent. The greatest threat to our society is civil war between these two groups. But nobody wants to know. The 'have-nots' are allowed to degenerate in ghetto areas that the 'haves' never visit. The only agency that reverses this drain is the church. Our church here is full of technocrats who love Jesus and love people. The result is that some of these no-hopers now share in our communal life; they are motivated, and some are moving into the world of technology themselves.'

The spiritual Nursery for a region

This visit made me think further about the ghastly gap between the ghettos and the technos. So when I heard

about a region newly named Mid Ambria, and its famed
Mid Ambria Nursery, I knew I had to go there. The Nursery filled a large valley, and consisted of a complex of
buildings surrounded by dairy, tree and fish farms and a
forest of wind-powered generators.

It turned out to be a nursery of human beings, not
plants. Some hundred people were the long-term members;
these had made life promises. About fifteen hundred were
in training or were testing out the possibility of making life
promises. Several thousand people who lived or worked in
the locality joined regularly in some of their activities or
worship, and fifty-six thousand Mid Ambria citizens were
enrolled as Friends.

Sharon was one of the Nursery's seven chaplains to
regional police forces. She accompanied young police
cadets in training and seasoned police on their beats, at
different times of day and night. The Nursery maintained
a twenty-four-hour emergency line so that any member of
the force who wanted confidential counsel could just ring.
Police officers felt able to cry and to be prayed for with the
Nursery folk, for they offered something no other agency
could offer. I discovered that there were chaplains to colleges,
football teams, leisure centres, factories, shopping centres
and social services. Some of the fittest, most able members
of the Nursery had been made chaplains to sink housing
estates. These were known as Motivators. In every case,
these chaplains had built up personal relationships with
the group they served, which in time had forged an ongoing
link with the Nursery. Some of these groups had their own
quarters at the Nursery, or had adopted a section of the
forest, the animal or the meditation farm. Those who
needed motivational training, and others recovering from
stress, stayed at the Nursery for up to several months. The

Nursery was self-supporting and many of the region's agencies made a financial contribution to it. Yet its new outreach work was done free of charge and contributions from many agencies remained voluntary. Recruits to the Nursery came from all styles of churches and each was encouraged to develop a distinctive talent, though this was based on a common discipline.

Ethnic churches and rainbow celebrations

Although Mid Ambria was being revitalised by its Nursery, I could not help wondering about regions whose ethnic groups were too divergent to bond with any one Nursery. So, as the cold and dark of Christmas approached I visited the most ethnically mixed metropolis in the country, and found myself entering a building bustling with Bangladeshis. Words from the Koran were read; everyone's shoes were piled in rows at the entrance. All were prostrate, facing east, for prayers. The story of Christ being born of a virgin was being read. A family was dressed as Mary and Joseph and the baby. 'Are you Christians or Moslems?' I asked a man as he finished his prayers. 'A Moslem means someone who obeys God so we are happy to be called Moslems,' he told me, 'I have not been baptised as a Christian yet. About 140 of us have our names on the list for baptism, but we wait until our whole family group is ready to be baptised. But most people here have already been baptised.'

As I explored this metropolis I found buildings where Chinese, Sikhs, Jews, Afros and many other ethnic groups had Christian worship in their own culture. 'How is it,' I asked a Sikh Christian, 'that your churches have the feel of the East more than of the West?' 'Many seekers of spirituality went East to find a spirituality, and dismissed

Christianity as a Western religion,' he beamed at me, 'but Jesus was not Western; Christianity is an Eastern religion. Our 'rainbow churches' visualise Jesus standing between East and West with his arms embracing each, bringing to fullness that which is eternally real in their traditions.'

I asked someone in another church: 'Each congregation is so different: how do you keep good relations between them?' 'We all sponsor the Rainbow Retreat,' she told me, 'when the elders of each congregation regularly listen to God together. Each congregation in turn hosts an annual Midsummer Rainbow Festival for everyone.'

The Real English Company

I returned in summer for the Rainbow Festival and struck up a conversation with a wise elder who had been born in Trinidad. 'The newer ethnic groups know how to celebrate together,' Siri told me, 'and now that so many of them are Christians they do it even better.' 'But what about the original English?' I ask. 'England is full of people who don't want to be English any more,' Siri said, 'in contrast to the other parts of the UK. The young try to be American, or anything rather than to be themselves. There is a crisis of identity.' 'So is Englishness gone for ever?' I ask.

'Not on your life,' Siri told me. 'It is most important that it finds a living, modern expression, otherwise the young English people will destroy their country. You must visit the Real English Company. One of their pubs is near here, and it's my favourite.'

Following a visit to the Real English Pub I found opportunity to drive to the Real English Company's headquarters in the west of England. The Company consisted of several hundred people. Most had enrolled for just one year; but some had enrolled for life. 'Life' meant one generation, since they figured that each adult could reckon on having three 'lives' in a 120-year life span.

If I had to choose one word to describe these folk it would be 'real', as in 'real ale' or 'real oak'. They were laid back, cheerful, in touch with themselves and their roots in their land. It soon became clear that they loved God a lot. The Company was sponsored jointly by the Church of England and the burgeoning Green Churches network. Their buildings consisted of a former minster church, which had become redundant, combined with an eco village of adaptable units which could easily change their shape and use. I learned that the Company owned a chain of Real English Pubs. These served Real Ale and Real English Worship, of both the minster and the folk variety. Many of their life members hosted these pubs, as a family or as groups of singles. These pubs thrived in areas that had long ago lost their old form of church.

The Company's Summer Academy drew people from far and wide, including those from deprived areas who came through a bursary scheme. I joined an introductory class who were discussing what it means to be English. Words and phrases like these were bandied about: Shakespeare, fish and chips, cricket, roast beef, strawberries and cream, football hooligans, bulldogs, Agatha Christie, pubs, minster churches, Ascot, Wimbledon, St George and merrie England, green hills, rose gardens, country churchyards.

Weren't most of these passé? I asked the course tutor, Alf Greenwood. 'They are surface images,' Alf agreed, 'but our course unearths the lasting treasure that is buried in our gene pool but which has been overlaid with junk.' 'I know how novices are inducted into Franciscan or Benedictine spirituality,' I rejoined, 'but how do you induct people into English spirituality?' Alf explained that the generation that spanned the Beatles and Princess Di had learned to speak what was in their hearts, rather than keep the stiff upper lip of the old southern English. But the post-modern generation was only in touch with surface wants and inchoate yearnings. The Company used the speak-from-the-heart approach, but helped students to unearth deeper and lasting aspirations.

Alf gave me a fascinating overview of the course: Aidan, the apostle of the English; Caedmon, the first English pop singer learning to celebrate God in creation; the Saxon sense of homely hospitality, friendship between men and women; Alfred the Great King and the qualities of magnanimity and bridge building; the English church as a bridge between Catholic and Protestant was traced from Alfred, through Queen Elizabeth I to modern times; the sturdy yeoman qualities and the ability to keep steady when all around is in turmoil; the English mystics; the Puritans; the hard work ethic and the entrepreneurial spirit; the Glastonbury legends and the pursuit of valour in Blake's 'green and pleasant land'.

Through the Company, the Green churches folk music revival, the Church of England's minster-style music and the Glastonbury tradition had come together. It was quite normal to see classic music scholars combining folk, Byrd and much else at the keyboard. I was told that often their pub churches would put out this notice: 'Anyone who wishes to prepare music for worship on Sunday please bring your instrument at . . . such a time'.

The Glastonbury Pop Festival, England's biggest, was now sponsored by the Company, which was in negotiation with the trustees of Glastonbury Abbey to sponsor an All England Festival every St George's Day. In fact, it had hopes of relocating its headquarters to the extensive Abbey site, developing self-catering accommodation for a hundred guests, and opening up the grounds to become a People's Peace Park, where wedding and other party picnics could be booked. At the centre would be the Chapel of Ceaseless Celebration, where music groups from around England would maintain a daily rota, celebrating God and the simple joys of creation. They hoped to establish a holistic healing centre under the oversight of the Trinity, a Creative Arts Centre, and a Body-Soul centre of Christian Prayer.

I came away wondering whether at last, after centuries, an Arthur-like leader might rise up who would help everyone to be truly English.

The Celtic experiments

Wales and Scotland never had the identity problem from which the English suffered. It was a delight to immerse myself in the Welsh Churches Alternative Eisteddfod. I was thrilled to spend three days at the All Scotland Christ Fest, and to discover the prayer movement which had swept through the mainline churches, producing all sorts of unexpected after-effects. There I met the young overseer of a scheme in which Catholic and Presbyterian churches jointly invested in pre-manufactured prayer chalets and training facilities at ancient holy sites.

The energising Christian communities I had encountered, however, were all in central places. A concern was growing in me for outlying places throughout Britain and Ireland, where many of the old churches had closed. The central Christian communities did service a large hinterland through their Internet outreach, but there were many people in neglected areas who never experienced Christian community.

I decided to do a survey. The old diocesan system of the Anglicans and Roman Catholics still existed on paper, though most bishops now lived in one of the inter-church faith communities. These, with their sophisticated computers, housed the archives of all the historic churches. I went to the archivist at one of these, and found a reference to a Bishop who, at the time many parishes and all the arch-deaconries in his diocese had been dissolved, had agreed to create an experimental parish in a Celtic style. A priest named Kevin, who had a family of five and innumerable pets, had asked the Bishop if he could pioneer such an experiment in a suitable place.

The Bishop had offered him St Hild's on the Marsh, a sprawling, tumbledown vicarage, which adjoined an old parish church and some glebe land. Two 70-year-olds in the tiny local hamlet acted as nominal churchwardens, someone did the flowers, and a local farmer cut the churchyard grass once a year. A couple in The Old Stables occasionally wandered round the building and said a prayer. The wealthy patron of the parish, who had kept the building in good repair, had recently died. That was all; there was no one else.

Kevin secured agreement that in future the patron would be the Community of the Saints, of which he was a member. If he became ill or had to move on, the community nature of the experiment was thus safeguarded. Second, St Hild's parish status would be annulled, so that it would be free from anachronistic regulations. There would be no salary, though the diocese would provide a starter grant, which would keep the family afloat for one year. The upkeep of the church building and vicarage would be the responsibility of the Community of the Saints.

Kevin began twice-daily family prayers and Friday open-house meals. Soon others joined the family, and emails arrived in response to his website asking if folk could join them. That's how the large garden evolved into a caravan and organic farm centre.

Evidently well over half the second-millennium dioceses had been amalgamated in a spirit of doom and gloom, but in the process, sometimes almost by accident, new experiments had taken off. For example, Newcastle Diocese was assimilated into Durham Diocese and Lindisfarne was made the Minster Church of the enlarged diocese. Every Christian who worked on the island signed a covenant that committed them to be in solidarity with the island, all its churches and its people who fished or farmed. Before long a large swathe of England and Scotland was revitalised by the Lindisfarne folk, and the fishing industry revived too.

Open churches with robots and hermits

Among the archives I learned of another experiment that was keeping churches alive in the wastelands. At the turn of the millennium there had been a short-lived Open Churches scheme supported by an impresario. This idea resurfaced when someone had the idea of robots who could keep church buildings open and secure throughout the day, hermit flats which could be pre-cast to fit into an existing church building and installed in a day and real hermits who kept living, daily prayer alive, and opened the premises as weekend retreat centres for families, businesses and leisure groups.

According to the archivist, St Hild's experiment had so impressed one bishop that he asked, before his diocese was subsumed in a larger one, whether his could become an experimental diocese. The sub-diocese was so transformed that all the church streams came together and there is now talk of subsuming the larger area into the smaller!

I felt someone beckon me to leave the archives and to walk out into the open air. I saw a breathtaking rainbow. It seemed to cover all of Britain and Ireland, and to touch the whole world with its sheen.

A bell rings. My dream comes to a sudden end. Work must begin.

CHAPTER 2

The Dying

Death: the final cessation of vital functions
in an organism.
Oxford English Reference Dictionary

Death can come by a thousand cuts. The shelf life of
second-millennium forms of church is nearing its end.
Anachronistic practices and mind-sets have accumulated
which make them alien to a majority of the population.

Although the gates of hell shall never prevail against the
essence of the universal church (Matthew 16:18), any particular form of that church can most certainly die. In his
travel book *From the Holy Mountain* William Dalrymple
observes many churches that have survived since the early
centuries but which are at this moment becoming relics.

The statistics of decline in Europe are well known and
remorseless. According to the *World Christian Encyclopaedia*
53,000 attenders are leaving the church in Europe and
North America every week.[1] Various more local surveys

1. Barrett, David B. (ed) *World Christian Encyclopaedia: A Comparative
Survey of Churches and Religions in the Modern World, AD 1900-2000*
(Oxford University Press, Nairobi, 1982).

conducted since 1982 indicate that if anything the decline is increasing.[2] The 1990 European Values Study showed that some 71 per cent claimed to believe in God, 68 per cent in the soul, and 54 per cent defined themselves as religious people. Active members of churches are 14.4 per cent of the population – regular churchgoing is under half that figure. Church of Scotland statistics published in the mid-1990s indicated that if the decline in membership continued, there would be no members left by the year 2024. The church is losing 18,000 members a year.

Many people think the Church of England is proceeding to die. Her obituary has already been written – mostly by people who have left the Church of England to join other churches.[3] The obituary goes something like this:

Requiem for the Church of England 1535-2005

After Henry VIII split from Rome, and some 300 people each side of the Protestant–Roman divide were executed for their beliefs, reaction followed counter-reaction. Political expediency eventually ruled the day and the great Anglican Compromise was put in place. This, however, was held together by the money, conventions and bureaucracy of the Establishment. It never had homogeneity. There was an Evangelical wing, a Catholic wing and a Liberal wing, each of which waxed and waned. In recent centuries the church became hostage to half-believing, culturally-elitist liberal bishops and lost the true marks of the holy, apostolic, catholic church. Bishops and clergy could disbelieve almost

2. See, for example, Grace Davie in *Religion in Britain since 1945: Believing without Belonging* (Blackwell Publishers, 1994).

3. See, for example, 'The Disintegration of the Church of England' in chapter 43 of *Orthodox Christianity and the English Tradition* by Fr Andrew Phillips (ISBN 1-898281-00-9 Published by the Anglo-Orthodox Trust).

anything and remain in place, morals became privatised and churchmanship became polarised. It was possible to meet two Church of England vicars who appeared to have nothing in common in their beliefs, dress, practices or morals. Increasingly the Church of England behaved like a sect, making decisions independently of the universal church. Because of the half-believing and Establishment mentality that was endemic in its diocesan structures, it lost the hearts and minds of the English people. As we moved into an age where people looked for integrity, coherence, community, mystery – it could offer none of these things. The bishops of the 1990s spent their energy planning how to decline efficiently, but numbers declined further, clergy became stressed out, and the church fragmented so much that Roman Catholics, New Churches and Muslims replaced it as the three largest religious groups in England. Finally it was beached, and formal disestablishment was merely a delayed epitaph.

There is nothing like execution to concentrate the mind. Before the funeral actually took place, an Archbishop of Canterbury (Dr George Carey) publicly faced the fact that a church can face extinction within one generation. His successor, Rowan Williams, called his flock to explore new ways of being church. The inherited Church, however, needs to fund the emerging Church. So it must start by discarding what hinders its mission.

RIP – what the retreating Church needs to discard

The retreating Church needs to discard attitudes and practices that have crept in, which were not of God, and which have put up barriers between the Church and the people. Prejudices, cloaked in the garb of doctrine, which may have helped people in previous cultures to understand the Faith, took the place of love and lack the suppleness that characterises living truth.

On the Holy Island of Lindisfarne pilgrim groups that consist of former churchgoers have asked me to dialogue with them. My friend John Sumner dialogues at Glastonbury with similar groups of former churchgoers. From such encounters we can draw up a list such as this:

Twenty things that make good people angry with the Church

Lack of humanity
Lack of integrity
Lack of spiritual depth
Lack of a generous spirit
Lack of tolerance of people who differ from them
Lack of forgiveness
Lack of imagination
Lack of awareness
Misuse of power
Engendering of false guilt
Mistreatment of the earth
Belittling of sexuality
Neglect of key life moments
Non-inclusive leadership
Misrepresentation of the nature of salvation
Misrepresentation of the nature of sin
Misrepresentation of heaven, hell and the other world
Wordy, preachy church services
Pressurised mission approaches
Abuse of power

John Sumner writes:

Fasten your seat belts.

We are seen to lack integrity. No, not the accusations of the sensational press, not the intolerance that expects clergy and Church to be perfect each twenty-four hours, not the guilt and hate that delights to see priests fall.

No, that hurts, but I don't mean any of that.
We stand accused of dishonesty in several ways:

Dishonesty in our reading of the Bible
Dishonesty in talking about God
Dishonesty in our assessment of others
Dishonesty in our assessment of wealth and power.

Post-modern people distrust big claims that do not connect with one's own experience. They reject judgemental words about others that do not connect with one's own vulnerability. They despise talk about love of neighbour by people and churches who do not connect with the poor.

RIP to God in the box

Organisms begin to die when they no longer respond to their environment. Richard Harries, Bishop of Oxford, has written about 'God outside the box'. Churches have become boxed in. The framework (the world view) in which they are set has changed out of recognition in the last 30 years. Some sociologists relate the emergence of 'new plausibility structures' to processes of religious change. P. L. Berger refers to the arrival on the world stage of new perspectives, elements and questions with regard to reality, existence and life itself, to which old religious explanations and structures no longer correspond.[4] The dying church relates to the old framework. The emerging church relates to the new.

We are entering a new age.

The European civilisation which we have known for the past two thousand years is giving way to a global civilisation.

Bede Griffiths

4. Berger, P. L. *Sacred Canopy* (Anchor Books, 1988).

A paradigm is the mental framework into which we fit everything we know. In most aspects of life – scientific, social, cultural, economic, ecological, psychological and religious – we no longer understand our world as did our forebears even until recently. The world and its institutions are going through the biggest shift for hundreds, perhaps thousands, of years.

This has profound implications for churches. All the second-millennium church streams have telltale signs of a mind-set that is becoming obsolete. This vast paradigm shift means that the form church has taken in the west for centuries now needs fundamental reappraisal.

RIP to a patriarchal Church

There is the possibility that religions, in the form that we know them, belong to the age of Patriarchy
(c. 8000 BC to 2000 CE).

Diarmuid O'Murchu [5]

Our culture is engaged in a tremendous reappraisal of the intuitive, of the feminine, of everything affecting or concerning subjectivity . . . Every indication exists that we are witnessing the emergence of one of the key archetypes of humanity's collective unconscious: the anima, in all of its multiple manifestations. A like event occurs only once every several thousand years.

And when it occurs, the axis of history suffers a universal shock, as men and women once more produce a new self-interpretation and redefine their interpersonal relations.

Leonardo Boff [6]

---

5. O'Murchu, Diarmuid *Quantum Theology* (Crossroad, New York, 1997)

6. Boff, Leonardo *The Maternal Face of God: The Feminine and Its Religious Expressions* (Collins, 1989).

The feminisation of society means that feelings have now won proper public respect alongside rationality. Sign, symbol and intuition are now seen to be essential to explain the whole dimension of reality. These need to be embraced, though negative aspects of feminisation such as gender confusion, crisis in masculinity and denial of motherhood also need to be addressed.

An article by Francis Fukuyama in *The Financial Times* was headed 'The Death of Hierarchy'. He argues that the flow of information is changing authoritarian forms of organisation in the workplace. They are being replaced by flat or networked organisations, where shared values are the key.[7] The patriarchal, top-down or one-shape-fits-all type of church has had its day.

RIP to a monochrome Church

Culturally accepted norms of a generation ago are now questioned. Some of these changes, especially as they affect a church context, have been expressed like this:

From	To
Monologue	Interaction
Cerebral	Visual
Consumerism	Simplicity
Explanation	Experience
Status	Service
Activism	Mysticism
Linear Thinking	Bit Thinking
Believing	Belonging
Argument	Story
Reductionism	Holism
Standardisation	Personal choice
External authority	Inner conviction

7. Fukuyama, Francis *The Weekend Financial Times,* 12/13 June 1999.

RIP to a non-ecological Church

> The western world is into a deep cultural pathology as we enter the terminal phase of the Cenozoic period.
>
> *Thomas Berry* [8]

Thomas Berry, the Roman Catholic Passionist priest, creationist and research director, calls for a massive shift from an anthropocentric to a biocentric view, if the planet is to survive as we know it. In recent decades a wide range of groups has emerged – conservationists, single-issue campaigners and those into deep ecology – who realise this truth.

RIP to a fragmented Church

The second-millennium forms of church are not only anachronistic, they are also fragmented. Few Christians under 40 want their identity to be tied to a protest movement that occurred over four hundred years ago, that is, to be labelled either Catholic or Protestant. We are living at the end of the era in which the Catholic/Protestant divide at the Reformation was the dominating framework of the western church. Christians are sensing that the Reformation represented not only a split in doctrine and organisation, but also a split in the western 'Christian' psyche. Now that the false splits between organisation and mysticism, between the whole and the parts, are beginning to heal in the corporate psyche, the churches have to catch up.

RIP to dehumanising tendencies

Second-millennium churches neglected the biblical Wisdom tradition in Christianity, which values the feminine in God

---

8. Berry, Thomas, CP, with Clarke, Thomas, SJ, *Befriending the Earth* (Twenty-third Publications, Mystic, Connecticut, 1991).

and in people. Towers, tasks and tirades became their landmarks. From the churches the people gained a vague impression that God was like a mean boss who tries to find out what people are doing in order to tell them not to.

Church people have been conditioned for centuries to disguise their innermost being. This point is tellingly made in Ronald Ferguson's biography of the Scottish Presbyterian minister George McLeod, who, he says, 'was keeping strict controls on access to his innermost core, where the puritan carefully policed the passionate. The language of one's innermost feelings was not in the McLeod family lexicon . . . he had the McLeod reputation of omni-competence to protect and uphold.'[9] After a breakdown George had a transforming experience, which enabled him thereafter to model a Christianity that helped people to become more fully human.

RIP to misuse of power

In his speech accepting the honour of a Union Medal from the Union Theological Seminary, New York, George McLeod said: 'The love of power has ruled the world, temporal and ecclesiastical, since the beginning of time. The Roman Empire was created by the love of power. The Roman Church got pre-eminence through the love of power. The love of power invaded John Knox in his desire to recover power for the new church [at the Reformation in Scotland]. Now science has given new meaning to power with nuclear weapons. Thus power has jettisoned

9. Ferguson, Ronald *George McLeod: Founder of the Iona Community*, p. 108 (William Collins, 1990).

morality. So this is indeed the Church's hour. Only one force is sufficient for our day. It is the power of love.'

C. J. Jung correctly diagnosed the future Nazi threat in Germany, because he understood that in that country's collective unconscious Christianity was a religion that had been imposed, and was therefore only on the surface. As a result, paganism, which had been repressed rather than redeemed, was poised to make a comeback in destructive new form.[10]

If we are to avoid the tragedy of an imposed, unnatural form of Christianity being replaced by a natural but unredeemed paganism we need to understand the context of our times:

Gardens of Love

I went to the Garden of Love,
And saw what I never had seen:
A Chapel was built in the midst,
Where I used to play on the green.

And the gates of this Chapel were shut,
And 'Thou shalt not' writ over the door;
So I turned to the garden of love
That so many sweet flowers bore.

And I saw it was filled with graves,
And tombstones where flowers should be;
And Priests in black gowns were walking their rounds,
And binding with briars my joys and desires.

William Blake

10. McLynn, Frank *Carl Gustav Jung* (St Martin's Press, New York, 1997).

RIP to defensive Church leaders

Why are so many Churches defensive rather than loving?

John Sumner writes of his experience of the training of leaders in his church:

> Unable to love myself, my capacity to love others is reduced. I have protective barriers between me and real human people. Videos, schemes, dress, housing, categorised ways of thinking, plans of Salvation, committee-made prayers.
>
> And because of my low self-confidence, I cannot see how to utilise the thoughts, the questions, the explorations, and the expertise of others who do not fit my trained schemes and thought-forms. We may have head teachers, speech tutors, senior managers, electronic technicians in our church, but I am so busy, so caught up in meeting ingrained expectations, that I cannot learn how to use them. We may have original thinkers, deep questioners, far-seeing spirits in our circle, but unless I can fit them into my system of concepts they had better be left unattended.

This negative experience was not universal among theological colleges. But I do believe it was widespread.

RIP to belittling of other religions

> I love all religions. I am in love with my own.
>
> *Mother Teresa of Calcutta*

E. Stanley Jones, the missionary to India, once asked Mahatma Gandhi: 'How can we make the Christian faith more native to India, so that it is no longer something "foreign" which is associated with foreign governments and seen as foreign religious practice, but it becomes part of life in India and a faith that makes a powerful contribution to building up this country?' Gandhi replied:

'Firstly, I would suggest that all Christians – missionaries and others – must start living more like Christ. Secondly, practise your faith without blurring it or watering it down. Thirdly, put special emphasis on love because it is the central point of Christian faith and therefore the decisive motivating force. Fourthly, study non-Christian religions with great sympathy, so that you can appeal to people of other faiths more effectively.'

RIP to denial

It is possible that what has already happened to traditional religious communities is now happening to churches. If so, we do well to heed what Gerald Arbuckle wrote in 1988:

> Many religious congregations today are in chaos. They are not sure about the meaning, contemporary relevance or mission of religious life and, on the practical level, they find it difficult to cope with often rapidly declining numbers, few or no vocations, and the rising average age of membership.
>
> Some congregations acknowledge that they are in chaos and are seriously concerned about wanting to do something about it. Others struggle to deny it, thinking it is just like a bad dream and very soon it will all disappear and 'things will be normal once more'. Other congregations, perhaps because they are still receiving vocations, e.g. in Third World countries, think they are not in chaos. They may in fact be in deep chaos, because they complacently refuse to search for the inner meaning of religious life and how it must respond with apostolic vitality to the pastoral needs of people today. They cannot at some point in the future escape the consequences of their prolonged denial.[11]

11. Arbuckle, Gerald A, SM, *Out of Chaos: refounding religious congregations* (Geoffrey Chapman, 1988).

We have to face up to the sea change that is taking place. This is affecting even the largest charismatic churches. The leader of one such church says, 'I can see it is dying underneath.'

Denominational leaders are saying that their present structures have only 10 to 20 years to survive. Then comes collapse. Will a phoenix rise from the ashes?

CHAPTER 3

The Longing

Two days after the death of Diana, Princess of Wales, the clergy of Bath and Wells Anglican Diocese were gathered with their bishop, Jim Thomson. He told them:

> The overwhelming sea of flowers and faces has told us of a yearning and an aching in the people of our lands. The people out there are not quite where we had thought them to be. It was the very complexities of Diana's make-up, her low points and her vulnerabilities, which evoked the sheer size of response. She was not coming from an emotionally privileged position. If she could do it, we could do it: the world wanted it.

> The people are not in the place we thought. And the churches are not heading where we like to think. The human being needs selfless and sensitive love, and the Christian commandment is to love. Though we may revise our liturgies, though we may devise schemes for the unemployed, though we may have study groups and Alpha groups and sound biblical scholarship, and have not love, we are doing nothing.

Diana had to accept that she could not be the official queen through formal means, but she became Queen of hearts. The world's mourning of her death marked a turning from hierarchy to the power of the heart. The church has to accept that it cannot influence people through status or formal powers; it has to become Queen of hearts.

Can the church change to fresh models? I believe it can for these reasons:

- A new generation of God-centred leaders is rising up.
- Change has been prophesied.
- A wave of fresh thinking is filtering through.
- Sorrow for past failings is bearing fruit.
- Realignments of Christian forces are gathering pace.
- There is a precedent for such change.

A new generation of leaders

I shall never forget listening to some prophetic church leaders at a packed London meeting. The gist of what I remember is this: 'The First World War destroyed a whole generation of leaders. In the period since then the church has had a dearth of both able and God-inspired leaders. Seventy years have now passed. The ancient people of Israel had to spend 70 years in exile in Babylon, but after this period they returned and began to fulfil God's plans again. Britain's churches have been in a kind of Babylon. That period is ending. There are now many humble leaders who desire God's will; God is equipping them to do great things . . .'

Young Christians are coming out of the woodwork in order to get training, some in established church centres, others in new frameworks.

Change is being prophesied

The poorly educated Welsh preacher Smith Wigglesworth, who raised several people from apparent death, said this in 1947:

> During the next few decades there will be two distinct moves of the Holy Spirit across the church in Great Britain. The first move will affect every church that is open to receive it and will be characterised by a restoration of the baptism and gifts of the Holy Spirit.
>
> The second move of the Holy Spirit will result in people leaving historic churches and planting new churches . . .
>
> When the new church phase is on the wane, there will be evidenced in the churches something that has not been seen before: a coming together of those with an emphasis on the Word and those with an emphasis on the Spirit. When the Word and the Spirit come together, there will be the biggest movement of the Holy Spirit that the nation, and indeed the world, has ever seen. It will mark the beginning of a revival that will eclipse anything that has been witnessed within these shores, even the Wesleyan and the Welsh revivals of former years. The outpouring of God's Spirit will flow from the UK to the mainland of Europe, and from there will begin a missionary move to the ends of the earth.

Rick Joyner[1], a contemporary USA prophetic leader, states: we are now entering one of the greatest watershed periods in human history. Creation itself is charged with the electricity of these times and is beginning to groan and travail for what is about to come . . . In preparation for this

---

1. Joyner, Rick, 'The Twenty-first Century Church' from *Prophetic Bulletin* (Morning Star Publications, PO Box 19409, Charlotte, NC 28219-9409, September 1999).

greatest of events the church is about to go through a metamorphosis. She is going to change from a worm into a butterfly. A caterpillar is confined to the earth, and its path must conform to the contour of the earth. Likewise, for nearly two thousand years the church has often conformed more to the ways of the world than to the ways of the Spirit.

Soon the church will go through a change so dramatic that she will seem to emerge as an entirely different creature. It will be like another birth . . .

A wave of fresh thinking

There has been a glut of books about the demise and the re-formation of the church. *Being Human: Being Church* by Robert Warren has challenged churches to turn into missionary congregations and into laboratories for becoming more fully human beings.[2] *O Brave New Church*, by Mark Stibbe, that brave vicar of St Andrew's, Chorleywood, diagnoses our society as a slave to various addictions. The church, too, has been addicted, he argues, but it is beginning to break free and become the agency, par excellence, which sets the people free from their addictions.[3]

In *New Tasks for a Renewed Church*[4] Tom Wright, now Bishop of Durham, urges Christians to find the focal points of the emerging new paganism, and to find ways of honouring Jesus as Lord within these contexts. He calls for Christian 'shrines' to be established in various areas: by

2. Warren, Robert *Being Human: Being Church* (Marshall Pickering, 1995).

3. Stibbe, Mark *O Brave New Church* (Darton, Longman & Todd, 1995).

4. Wright, Tom *New Tasks for a Renewed Church* (Hodder & Stoughton, 1992).

coming alongside those in pain as a result of war; by proclaiming in liturgy and deeds that the powers of Mammon shall be brought low and the needy shall be lifted up; by celebrating sexuality as the glory of a relationship of integrity; by cherishing the earth; by developing forgiving and respectful friendships with people of other faiths within which witness becomes authentic; by restoring the Eucharist and a sacramental approach to the centre of church life; by rescuing from eastern monopoly the mystical and contemplative traditions of prayer; and by restoring holism to intellectual endeavour.

In *Threshold of the Future: Reforming the Church in the Post-Christian West,* Michael Riddell gives examples of churches in his native New Zealand which are pioneering new ways of being Church, from Parallel Universe to Spine.[5]

In a Rural White Paper in 2000 the UK Government sought to enlist church buildings and staff to deliver vital public needs in rural areas. *The Times* of 4 September 2000 commented: 'A better adapted breed of clergy . . . can return the Church to its medieval role as the linchpin of a community . . . The halls where pensioners shiver after Sunday service . . . could double up for the rest of the week as post office premises, as social clubs for the elderly, as crèches for the working mother.'

5. Riddell, Michael *Threshold of the Future: Reforming the Church in the Post-Christian West* (SPCK, 1998).

Also:

Monagh, Michael *Changing World: Changing Church* (Monarch Books, 2001).

Repentance for the Church's past sins

As the second millennium drew to a close, some churches tried to identify significant wrong actions in the second millennium that lived on in distorted patterns, to say sorry and to put right what could be put right. They followed the example of Ezra and Nehemiah in the Old Testament.

If Christianity is to be a force for healing the world in the third millennium, the image of the Cross as a sword by which people of other faiths are forced to convert against their will, must be expunged and it must become again, as it was at the beginning, an image of unconditional love. Pope John Paul II called on his church to make penance for their mistreatment of Jews.

For millions of Muslims and Jews, the Cross symbolises the sword. So it is a wonderful thing that Christians from various backgrounds have made Reconciliation Walks along the routes Crusaders took through Muslim lands to pray, to say sorry, to make friends. Mothers and children ran over to these walkers with tears and embraced them. A whole new set of dynamics was coming into play. If Christianity is experienced as a movement of unconditional love, who knows how far the healing of fragmentation may go in the Muslim and Christian worlds?

Churches in Australia took part in a 'National Sorry Day', in which schools and organisations throughout the land said sorry to the aboriginal people for the raping of their land and culture by the European invaders.

South Africa's Truth and Reconciliation Commission, headed by Archbishop Desmond Tutu, was an historic example of this corporate healing process. The Anglican Church in Japan, at its synod in 1996, formally confessed its sin in having supported their country's colonial war of oppression in World War II. It says its first synod after the war 'should have deeply repented for not having fulfilled their prophetic role. They should also have made a sincere apology to their neighbours whom Japan had invaded and ruled, and should have sought a truly reconciled relationship with them . . .'

As pilgrims from Roman, Anglican, Reformed and New Church traditions gathered at Lindisfarne in 1997 during their journey from Rome to Iona, a confession in the following vein was made:

> We confess with shame
> > the loss in the Church of integrity, humility and patience
> > the crushing of spontaneity
> > the caging of the wild Spirit
> > the breaking off of relationships
> > the bruising of the crushed reeds
> > the arrogance of the intellect
> > the pride of empire-building.
>
> We accept our share of responsibility for these sins,
> > and seek to shed them on behalf of ourselves and our churches.
> > Lord, have mercy upon us and forgive us.

Realignments are taking place

A man walked into my cottage: 'Can I talk to someone about how to make my faith more real? I feel that it must mean more than just going to church on a Sunday. I have talents to offer the church, but where I live nobody wants to know.' Andrew turned out to be skilled in IT and communication. The business world took him seriously and paid him well. The church, which could have had his services free, had no use for him. Why? Because the church tried to fit people into its narrow framework of Sunday liturgy; it did not facilitate God's gifts in its members and let these become an expression of its life and witness. Andrew's story can be repeated countless times.

I said to Andrew: 'If you were a member of a political party, and your local branch was dominated by fuddy duddies, would you leave that party or link up with the live regional or national networks of that party? Think of the church in a similar way. I will try to help you find the right network.' That began an adventure for Andrew. That part of his story, too, can be repeated increasingly. It is possible to move out of narrow straitjackets into creative networks that are part of the wider Body of Christ.

There is a precedent for radical and successful change in our own history

Some church leaders (including Anglo Catholic, Pentecostal, Orthodox and Roman Catholic) still insist that theirs is the only 'true' model of church. There are many more who recognise that external church patterns are becoming obsolete but who doubt whether a new-fangled model of church can bear the weight that will be put upon it and still remain authentic. By rediscovering our hidden but deepest roots, new church is able to grow up within as well as alongside the old church.

That is what the next chapter explores.

CHAPTER 4

The Birthright

'We are coming to the end of the parish phase of church,' said Bishop Ian Harland, 'it has happened before.'

People who realise that the second-millennium form of church has no future nevertheless fear lest it should be replaced by new-fangled forms of church that are not deeply rooted.

Saint Patrick introduced the top-down diocesan system into fifth-century Ireland, for that was all he knew from his training in the urban centres of the continent. Yet within a hundred years the focus had changed from the bishop to the monastery, which was led by a man or a woman. Bishops continued their sacramental duties, but they were under the authority of the abbot, who looked after the organisation. The pattern of church organisation followed the natural pattern of the people groups.

One ruling family after another embraced the Faith and gave prime parts of their estates to be used as monasteries, which became the hub of the tribal life. These early monasteries had no barriers, apart from a ditch for practical reasons. There was constant movement in and out by children, women, labourers. There were no imposing buildings.

These monastery churches were multi-functional resource centres. They served as prayer base, drop-in centre, library, school, health centre, psychiatric care centre. They were totally open to outsiders. To them visitors brought the news of the world. They related to the neighbourhood as guardians of local culture, affirming it whether it was vibrant or dying, though confronting certain bad practices such as wizardry.

Even within the monasteries there were all sorts of options. There were clergy, lay monks and nuns with life vows, others with temporary vows, and some who lived at home. Some were married.

The major Celtic monasteries were not built, as were the eastern ones, as an escape from the world. They were built on the main highways of sea and river and near large settlements; they were organised in order to penetrate the pagan world and to extend the church.

The monasteries provided a God-given framework of prayer, work and rest, reflecting the rhythms of the natural and the Christian year. They were the main centres of hospitality and Celtic Christians were taught to 'open their heart to Christ in the stranger'. They also introduced written education to Ireland.

Some became learning centres. Others offered 'perennial praise'.

At Bangor over 3000 monks devoted themselves to the singing of Perennial Praise. Their praise book, the Bangor Antiphonary, which is preserved in the Ambrosian library, Milan, says, 'Let the many keep awake in community on a third of the nights in the year in order to read aloud from the Book and to expound judgement and to sing blessings all together.'

The early monastic churches marvellously modelled hospitality. The eighth-century Rule of St Ailbe suggested that hospitality should consist of 'a clean house, a big fire, a good wash and a comfortable bed.' Some Celtic churches, such as Columba's monastery at Durrow, fed a thousand visitors a day.

The monastic churches in Ireland and in Saxon Britain were a source of soul friendships. Bede says those outside the monasteries flocked to Aidan, Cuthbert, Hilda. So also they did to David of Wales.

Columba went into exile from the security of his beloved homeland and founded the Iona monastery on Scotland's western shore. True, this was a strategic place, but it was also on the edge. From the extremity of Iona, Aidan brought a mission to English barbarians, and established his church base on borderland between isle and mainland at Lindisfarne. The many daughter churches he planted throughout the large kingdom of Northumbria, though inland, kept alive that same borderland spirit. Thus Cuthbert and Eata, transferred from one Lindisfarne daughter church at Melrose to another at Ripon, were edged out when the Romanising prelate Wilfred took control, and having no worldly handles, returned to Melrose. Bede wrote of those Lindisfarne servants of Christ: 'None of them would accept lands or possessions to build monasteries, unless compelled to by the secular authorities.'

Why did people throng to the early Celtic communities, in Britain as much as in Ireland? The whole life of the monk, his service to guests, his work, his prayer, silence, rest, relations with his brothers, were offered as a liturgy to the Holy Trinity. The physical pattern of the monastery bore witness to this reality. From the church and its holy altar all things proceeded, and to them all things returned. The huts, the refectory, the guest room, everything revolved around the hub, which was the place of worship. Worship was repeated each day and night, yet, for those who entered into it from the heart, it was not static. It was a single motion towards God; it had an inner dynamic which reflected God's rhythms and by which the soul moved upwards towards God, and raised all creation.

Monasteries in Britain were not otherworldly. Animals and children would wander around. In Anglo-Saxon England, monasteries became the nearest thing to a town.

It was only later that pride of power and possessions, that ugly sore that hid under the veneer of religion, strutted across the church. The continual repentance of the heart, the daily immersion in Christ's Eucharistic self-giving, the sharing of goods in common, became a distant memory.

Hermitage churches

Hermits went to the edges of rocks or lakes, and churches sprang up around them. Kevin, the tall skin-wearing hermit of Glendalough, chose to live in a sunless cave 50 feet above a lake inhabited by a wild creature; it was as if he needed to reach to the extremity of life in order to find the all-sufficiency of God. Around Kevin's cave grew up the seven churches of a monastic city.

A Breton *Life of St Gildas* tells how his sister and two of his brothers established a *skete* in a remote place. Each had their own dwelling and their own place of prayer, some distance apart. Each brother took it in turns to spend much of the day with his sister, sharing in the regular hours of prayer, Holy Communion, a meal, and no doubt in work or vigils. Each of the three returned to their own place before sunset and kept vigil there. Evidently all sorts of people were drawn to them, for the author of *The Life of Gildas* says they became famous for their constant miracles. No constant miracles without people![1]

The hermitage, or *skete*, was an alternative model to the central monastic church, and became widespread in Britain and in Ireland. The original intention was not to establish a hub church in an accessible place, but to find a quiet place in which to serve God in an undisturbed rhythm of prayer and work. The by-product was that, by a mysterious chemistry, people who were tuned in to this life of deep peace were drawn to these places. They made their own dwellings in the same area, adopted a similar lifestyle, and shared in Holy Communion and meals on certain festival days. As years passed these became pilgrim centres and a form of church, which met the need of many.

The Celtic Church was culture-friendly

None of the Celtic Christians who won over the indigenous population were martyred. This was not because they feared or favoured, but because they harnessed all that was gospel-friendly in their culture to Christ.

'In Christ are hidden all the treasures of wisdom and knowledge' (Colossians 2:3). Celtic Christians incorporated wisdom from the Druids, who had the wisdom of nature. The Celtic missionaries said God had given people two books, the book of Scripture and the book of creation. The Druids had a deep intuition. There is an Irish story that on the day of Christ's crucifixion King Conchubar noticed the

---

1. *The Life of Gildas* was probably written by a monk at the monastery of Rhuys, Brittany in the ninth century. See *Two Lives of Gildas* translated by Hugh Williams (Llanerch, 1990).

eclipse of the sun and asked the Druid Bucrach the cause of this sign. 'Jesus Christ, the Son of God, who is now being crucified by the Jews,' replied the Druid. Christians recognised that the intuition of their best forebears was in tune with Christ even before they had been taught about him. The sixth-century Welsh bard Taliesin declared: 'Christ, the Word from the beginning, was from the beginning our teacher . . . there never was a time when the Druids of Britain held not its doctrines.' As a baptised boy, Columba was taught by a Druid; as an adult he supported measures to strengthen the institution of the bards, yet he tried to lead both Druids and their pupils to Christ. 'Christ is my druid,' he told them. Later it was the Irish monks who first wrote down the pre-Christian folk stories, which continued traditional wisdom.

The Irish were led to transfer their veneration from the High King of Ireland to the High King of Heaven; from the sun to the Sun of suns. On standing stones in Ireland Christians placed an arrow to lead the passer-by from the sun disc, which pagans had engraved on one side, to the disc of Christ transcending the sun, which Christians had engraved on the other side. Christ is placed in the centre of the sun circle on most old Christian Celtic crosses.

Celtic believers Christianised the pagan seasons. The pagan blessing of the lustral waters on 6 January became the Epiphany, which commemorated Jesus' immersion in the waters. Candles were held to the throat for healing on the first day of the Celtic Spring, and this became St Brigid's Day. Christians continued the Druids' use of ashes as a sign of purification. The veil between earth and heaven was at its thinnest on Samhain, the first day of winter's dark: Christians filled it with the splendour of All Saints' Day.

The early church assimilated Greek wisdom and Celtic

Christians incorporated wisdom from the Druids. Our church has to assimilate the wisdom of the best neo-pagans of today.

We, who for the first time since those days live in a predominantly pagan population, do well to learn from the Celtic Christians, who in effect said to their pagan contemporaries: 'Come with your festivals that celebrate the elements, and we will transform them into festivals for the Lord of the elements. Come with your long, flowing hairstyles – when we become Christian monks we will keep these hairstyles because they give glory to God. Come with your clans and natural networks of association, and we will plant Christian communities of prayer that go with the grain of these networks. Come with your excitement about the Afterworld, but let us see how the risen Son of God throws light upon it. Come with your hunger for worship and the world of the Spirit, and we will explain how idols have no place now, because the God of gods has revealed himself to us . . .'

Their leaders

The leaders of monastic churches were the natural leaders of the people. They were usually members of extended ruling families who made a life commitment to Christ. There were exceptions. Ciaran was the son of a carpenter, but his physical and spiritual stature was so exceptional that Columba thought the whole of Ireland would follow him. He founded the monastic church at Clonmacnoise, which flourished for a thousand years.

Women leaders were given equality of regard in the church. The leaders of the early large monasteries for both women and men were invariably women. The manner in which male church leaders addressed their female counter-parts in the Celtic period is that of brother to sister.

The Saxon minster model

The Anglo-Saxons continued the monastic churches, and many of them had the feel of a family. An information board at Brecon Cathedral, Wales, describes how, before the Normans took over, the cathedral was a mother community to a network of smaller churches. These were known as a *clas*, meaning that they were part of one family.

The Saxon monasteries, however, were increasingly regulated by bishops with a territorial responsibility – and people with inspirations for fresh monastic churches could not follow the patterns of the people as easily as before. The scholar monk Bede recommended that Bishop Ecbert should put down monasteries that did not toe the line with his diocese. This was a contrast to the bishops in the Celtic Mission, who placed themselves under the authority of an abbot and who did not have the power to veto monastic developments.

A focus for the multiplying churches in Saxon Britain was the minster. This was a large church building that was both a multi-resource centre and a community of clergy and other helpers who serviced the outlying churches. It was, of course, tied in to the national church's chain of command, and it perhaps became too clericalised over time; but it is a model that is being looked to again.[2]

It was the Normans (1066 and All That) who finally obliterated the sense of the inclusive, grass roots family in the church. The tone of church leaders after the Norman Conquest was quite different. Much of the post-Norman

2. Cavill, Paul *Anglo-Saxon Christianity* (Fount, 1999) explores this, though rather uncritically.

Ancrene Wisse (Guide for Anchoresses), for example, is written so that women shall know their place in a masculine hierarchy and society. [3]

The modern rediscovery of Celtic-style churches

In his book *The Celtic Way of Evangelism: How Christianity can reach the West . . . Again,* George Hunter III of Asbury Theological Seminary, USA, argues that the Reformed churches, as well as the Roman Catholic churches of the USA, have continued the 'Roman paradigm' with dire results. He thinks that most leaders of America's churches are in denial, and continue to assume that control from headquarters, and the culturally European paradigm, are best for churches everywhere. He believes that if western church leaders 'are willing to learn from a once-great Movement outside of the Roman paradigm, then Christianity can become contagious once more across North America and Europe in the twenty-first century.'[4]

Ordinary people are often more apt to pick this up than are their church leaders.

> We never knew this existed, but it's what we've always thought.
> We've always felt there is something more.
> We've been so oppressed by the Roman ways of the church.
> It's the natural way to live for people in this land.
>
> *Joe O Siorain, leader of an Irish pilgrim group*

This desire to recover a Celtic style of church is spreading across the world. I receive many letters and emails that

3. Fell, Christine *Women in Anglo-Saxon England and the Impact of 1066* (British Museum Publications, 1984).

4. Hunter, George *The Celtic Way of Evangelism* (Abingdon Press, USA, 1999).

indicate this. 'Having found this Celtic way of life I realise that is what I've always believed, but this has put it into words for me. I never knew it existed. Why didn't the church tell me?' wrote one person, 'Can you tell me of any church that follows this way?'

In the USA Tom Sine, the author and Christian Futures Consultant, aims to develop a Celtic-style community led by three couples, where students can gain an experience of living in a rhythm of prayer, work, study and relationship. A church leader from Austin, Texas identifies a similar need. In order to 'detoxify' people from 'the disease for degrees', which treats people as if they are not valid unless they accumulate paper certificates, she seeks Celtic-style centres where people learn in a holistic, unpressured way through experience, prayer, relationship, intuition, as well as from books.

From Australia, church planter Brad Bessell writes:

Under our South Australian desert is the great artesian basin filled with millions of litres of water. The same could be said about the soul of this nation. It seems that church here looks for its nourishment from the seasonal rains that blow in from other countries. It comes and it goes and the land (church) is dry again. I believe that the Celtic Spirituality is not a seasonal rain or trend but something that is deeply buried under the Australian soul like our artesian waters under the desert. It is in the blood of the Scottish, Irish, Welsh, English convicts and immigrants. It just needs to be tapped. I believe that the role of Celtic Spirituality in this nation is to bring healing and reconciliation between the Aboriginal and Non-Aboriginal. In fact, I believe that had Celtic monks come to Australia instead of convicts etc. then the Aboriginal people would have had a spiritual experience similar to that of the ancient Celtic Christian. I also believe the role of the

Celtic renewal in this nation is to encourage the Church to embrace a faith that is more gentle and incarnational than the colonial one that we have inherited from our English forebears and less 'salesman' like than the recent American models that we seem to have embraced.

Clergy come to Lindisfarne in search of this new way. They arrive as *aparatchiks*, rushing from pillar to post. They yearn to become people who are tuned in. Some establish a daily pattern of stillness and prayer. Others already have this, but it has become an insulation from the rest of the day, rather than a way of being fully present to God and to others, throughout the day.

The well-known conference speaker David Pawson issued a cassette entitled 'de-Greecing the church', in which he complains about the pagan influence of neo-Platonism on the early church via Augustine of Hippo. After listening to this, a Cambridge scientist wrote: 'His complaints exactly echo your own complaints about what happened to the Celtic church following Augustine of Canterbury. The dynamism of Celtic Christianity is therefore precisely that of what is called "the early Church" (i.e. in Mediterranean lands).'

Lessons we can draw from these early models

We cannot, of course, recreate the organisation of the early Celtic church, nor should we. But it is possible to learn from them. It was Archbishop Michael Ramsay, quoting Arnold Toynbee, that great historian of the rise and fall of civilisations, who distinguished between historical movements based on archaism, and those based on transfiguration. As we grasp something of the mindset and dynamic of the Church in Celtic lands, we can move forward in a way that transforms.

The nature of Celtic-style churches today

How much of what is meant by 'Celtic-style church' today actually correlates with what existed in the church of the fifth-tenth centuries is a matter of debate. Documents are fragmentary, much is not certain, and in any case opportunities then were more limited. This does not invalidate the use of the term 'Celtic' as a symbol for today. For symbols accrue energies, and some key features of the early church in Celtic lands have become symbols, which now bear their own life.

What do people mean by a Celtic-style church? I often say that Celtic-style churches have the three R's: rhythm with God, roots in the land, rapport with the people. There is growing consensus that Celtic-style churches weave together biblical, charismatic and catholic strands.

Are they for cities? Yes, for Celtic-style churches make connections between their surroundings and God, and are fully attentive to whoever and wherever they are. Wherever there can be a rainbow overhead, there a Celtic-style church can be.

The following collection of attributes is drawn from all sorts of workshops and conversations.

CELTIC-STYLE CONGREGATIONS ARE

+

in God
holistic
grassroots
hospitable
communal
endogenous
non-sectarian
culture-friendly
creation-friendly
creative and poetic
deep but not overlaid
at home with the body
concerned for the poor
single-minded in mission
disciplined yet spontaneous
rhythmic in prayer and work
adaptable to their environment
genuine towards other churches
heartfelt and natural in worship
simple and uncluttered in life-style
familiar with the world of the Spirit
in continuity with the original church
incarnational without being parochial
at peace with neighbours and animals

THEY ARE FREE FROM

clutter and artificiality
legalism and clericalism
wordy, stereotyped worship
hidden or defensive agendas
triumphalist or competitive attitudes

Roots for renewal

A person who is secure in their roots is free to explore the future. So is a church.

The Old Testament Church had roots in the land and in the saving acts of God in its people. First-millennium churches had roots in their Jewish parentage and in the apostles of their own lands.

An endogen is a plant in which new wood is developed in the interior of the stem: an endogenous church grows within the life of the people of its land. The last time the churches of Britain and Ireland were truly endogenous was the period of the Celtic Mission.

We have already observed how second-millennium churches became disconnected from the grassroots patterns of the people, from the communal memory and from the earth itself. Third-millennium churches will reconnect with these.

Jung helps us understand the collective unconscious of peoples. For example, he understood Germany as a country of two levels. The surface level was Christian, but since Christianity had originally been forced upon it at the point of a sword, this was thin. The lower level was the pagan gods, which, taking vengeance after Germany was humiliated at the Treaty of Versailles, would now break the bonds of its underground prison and take over, wreaking terrible havoc.

Hitler plugged into the collective unconscious of 78 million Germans. The emerging church has to plug into the collective unconscious, not to repress its basic instincts, but to transform them.

CHAPTER 5

Features of the Emerging Church

Listening and journeying

The church of the Old Testament was a people on the move, who listened to God for direction. Although the desert travel phase ended, they habitually sang songs of ascent on the way up to the temple. Their temptation, like ours, was to get stuck, but prophets constantly urged them to walk humbly with their God. The members of the New Testament church were first called followers of the Way (Acts 9:2). Indeed, Church tradition recognises the importance of journey. In some places the Rite of Initiation into the Roman Catholic Church is popularly known as 'The Journey'.

In the new way of being church, programmes and buildings are provisional; they flow out of Spirit-led initiatives and when that tide ebbs, they are beached. Thus there is space to hear God for the new thing God wants to do.

Churches that live in this way are not afraid to cross new frontiers. Sometimes this means asking God to show them an opportunity they are meant to take or a need they are meant to respond to.

The British composer John Tavener, who was converted to the Orthodox Faith in 1976, says that the churches of the West will be unable to recover their mission until they recover humility, which he feels the churches of the East have not lost in the same way. One way the Western churches can recover this humility is to recover the idea of pilgrimage as a way of mission as well as of life. Celtic Christians went into exile from the safety and power zones of their home church in order to walk with nothing but Jesus in their hearts. Because they were so vulnerable, so mobile and so full of Jesus, many of the pagans they befriended became Christians. John Finney, in his book *Recovering the Past: Celtic and Roman Mission*[1] concludes that more people became Christian this way than through organised missions. The church historian David Edwards asserts that 'Europe was changed by these pilgrims for the love of God.'

This trait of the emerging church can synchronise with post-modern culture. In an abbreviated version of his *The Ties that Bind Us* Matthew D'Ancona wrote in *The Times Magazine* of 18 May 1996 about a study on Swindon, which lacks population stability or focus. D'Ancona concludes: 'In ways mundane and intriguing, the people of Swindon are learning to live with modernity which one of them described as "the vagabond way". In their unhistoric acts are lessons for us all, gathered on this uncertain vagabond pilgrimage to the Britain of the future.'

One church leader tells me that his congregation has two types of people: position people, who know what their position is and are against receiving from anyone who does

1. Finney, John *Recovering the Past: Celtic and Roman Mission* (Darton, Longman & Todd, 1996).

not hold it; and boom and bust people, who have an experience of the Spirit, then take time out when it goes wrong. He wants to bring a third sort into being: the person who receives from God and mentors others.

In his book *Life After God* Douglas Copeland quotes young people who ask questions such as, How can I fly? How can I have friends? How can I enjoy Christians without the pain of church? Copeland's suggestion is: have safari tours round the homes of Christians.[2]

I have been told of churches in USA who take youngsters away climbing, walking, etc. They are each given a staff, newly cut. As they walk they talk freely about their childhood; they are free to ask questions about their sexuality, money, anything. They are encouraged to talk about what they have found difficult as infants, juniors, at home, with parents, peers, schools. Each time they become aware of something important to their journey they mark it on their staff. In the evenings they will talk about these. And pray. Before they leave they will throw their staff on to a fire to be burned. In this way they marked that they are leaving their childhood. They make a commitment to Christ.

A church in Birmingham set up a 'Voice of the People' Trust. The Revd Dr Laurie Green, Principal of the Aston Clergy Training Course, wrote of this:

> The 'Voice of the People' . . . comes from a deeply felt Christian concern that since all of us are made in God's image, then we should all be listened to . . . The 'Voice' tries to act as a vehicle for working class values and working class culture to be expressed . . . The powers that be will learn a lot from listening to the Cry of the City just as in the Bible, time and again, it was the cry of the people at

2. Copeland, Douglas *Life After God* (Simon & Schuster, 1995).

the bottom of the pile that was the voice that God listened to and upon which God acted.

Many residents perceive the local church as a privatised concern for a minority. They do not feel the church is in solidarity with their good, even though non-religious, aspirations. Businesses and political parties conduct listening exercises in order to respond more effectively to the people they are trying to reach, so is there any good reason why we churches should not listen?

Raymond Fung, Evangelism Secretary of the World Council of Churches, was urging churches to draw up an agenda with people of goodwill in the neighbourhood. He called this an Isaiah Agenda, because passages such as Isaiah 65:20-23 provide examples of agendas of justice and peace that require partnership with the population.[3]

In Bowthorpe (see chapter 7), our leaders explored how we might harness the following modern equivalent of Isaiah's agenda to the local population:

- Every child cherished from conception.
- Every old person living and dying in dignity.
- Every person having a place of their own and fruitful work.
- Joy and safety in the streets.
- Trust between age- and ethnic-groups.
- Harmony with the environment and God.

When a church truly listens to the cries of the people and to the cries of its God it becomes, in the words of Dr Philip Potter, a former President of the World Council of Churches, the prophetic conscience of society.

3. Fung, Raymond *How a Local Congregation Evangelises and Grows* (World Council of Churches).

A daily rhythm of prayer, work and re-creation

> To my mind, tradition is a God-given awareness of natural
> rhythms and of a fundamental harmony.
>
> *Prince Charles*

Tragically, the worship of most churches consists of packaged words that do not so much as say hello to the sun's dawning, the rain's falling, or the day's dying. Or else the worship spills out of the psyches of dominant members who are too surfeited to notice the rhythms of their own bodies, let alone of the days or the years. Yet it is possible to create a sense of daily rhythm which touches and inspires a wider number, even among the most mobile populations, and which connects them with the ebb and flow of deeper realities.

The Bible sets the entire story of God's saving work for humanity within the setting of a universe of rhythm. The Bible tells how God chooses a people and teaches them ways of reflecting that rhythm in their society: through one day in seven and one year in seven, rest; the rhythm of prayer that reflects the sun rising, the sun at its midday height and the sun setting. The New Testament presents Jesus as the model for human beings, living a rhythm of total self-giving to the people and total withdrawal to a solitary place. The Saviour arranged for his most significant actions to coincide with the rhythm of the religious seasons.

In emerging churches the corporate worship follows the rhythm of the natural seasons and of the church year, and observes seasons of fasting or spiritual warfare, of lamentation for the sins and hurts of society, and of joy and celebration of creation.

The word rhythm comes from a Greek word (rhuthmos), whose root meaning is flow. Physicists are discovering that our universe has an underlying pattern; nature is full of symmetry. Rhythm is indivisible. There is a rhythm of the seasons of the year, and a rhythm of the seasons of life. There is a rhythm between masculine and feminine. The emerging churches seek to flow in these rhythms.

Mike Bream, of St Thomas Church, Crookes, Sheffield, calls his church to a holiday period in July and August because that is the natural thing to do. Then it has more energy to develop programmes in the new autumn season.

Many things in life can be harnessed to rhythm. West Indian bands harness modern technology to serve their rhythmic music. Cassian's Institutes, Section 2 reveals that in monastic worship a cantor would sing 10 verses of a psalm while everyone else listened; this was followed by silent prayer and a collect. There were four cantors who took turns to sing the psalms.

The first Council of the New Testament churches saw these as a restoration of King David's set-up, and a making good of the gaps in it (Acts 15:16). This, without doubt, included the restoration of daily worship.

> If this daily offering of total worship does not again become the centre of our life, our world will not be able to be transfigured or united. It will be incapable of surpassing its divisions, its imbalance, its emptiness and death, in spite of all human-centred plans to improve it.
> *Archimandrite George Capsanis of Mount Athos*

In the first millennium the daily prayer together in the larger, hub churches was normal, and these were called 'People's Services'. However, they degenerated. Monastic churches developed long, wordy services that suited celibate monks but which put off the general population. Daily worship in central churches became clericalised, form became more important than fellowship, ritual more important than relationship. A counter-church culture developed which encouraged prayers from pulpits or in groups, but not corporate daily prayer.

In the third millennium, we have to make good the gaps, integrating the creativity and spontaneity of occasional prayer gatherings, with the first millennium's rhythm of corporate daily prayer. This is beginning to happen, in churches of all shapes and sizes. Some use Anglican or Roman Catholic liturgies. Others use simpler, more flexible patterns. Daily prayer patterns from contemporary communities such as Aidan and Hilda, Iona, Northumbria and Taizé are increasingly being adopted.

Hospitality

> The fundamental need of our society is to have men and women who together create communities of welcome.
>
> *Jean Vanier*

Lack of hospitality has been the constant charge of God against his people. Many churches welcome newcomers at the door on Sunday, but these are not welcomed into the other rooms, as it were, during the week. Twentieth-century churches tended to welcome people as believers: emerging churches welcome them as neighbours.

In a people's church there is a welcome throughout the week, a place to be alone, to pray, to share a meal, to be listened to. There are displays and facilities that children, old people, business people, deaf people, can relate to.

I have often asked church leaders if they know of churches that feed a thousand people a day, as did Columba's church at Derry. They have told me of Sikh temples that do this, but not of a Christian church. Nevertheless, a growing number of churches do sponsor lunch clubs, refreshments or cafés. Many of these are not, however, part of a whole experience. In a monastic-style church, lunch guests do not have to leave when the lunch club closes, they can stay to pray, wander, study or talk to people who are always there, in the atmosphere of a spiritual home.

The early British churches hosted the main social events in their area. All who lived and worked in the vicinity of the monastic church would be welcomed to the large barn with a blazing fire and an instrument would be passed round. Each could take a turn to sing or play. The modern equivalent to this is the karaoke. Generally, pubs host these rather than churches. Emerging churches will host karaokes, barbecues and firework evenings.

I shall never forget touring Poland in the 1980s. Despite the fact that it was then behind the Iron Curtain, large numbers of young Catholics from other countries traversed the land with rucksacks on their backs and slept on the floors of church halls, where they also used the kitchen and wash facilities. This contrasts with Britain, where the youth hostel movement is divorced from the church. People's churches have hostels.

Hospitality is not only about accommodation; it is also about creating emotional space. People who have ceased to go to churches now go to retreat houses. The reason, according to Paddy Lane of the National Retreat Association, is that retreat houses provide them with a welcoming, safe context where that which is of God in them can be drawn out; whereas churches put upon them sermons, hymnbooks, noise and churchy agendas. Monastic-style churches provide both physical and emotional space.

Hospitality is a sign that a community is alive, that it is not afraid, that it has something valuable to share. To welcome anyone is always a risk: an over-busy community that opens its doors can become a burned-out community.

There is a time for a community, as for an individual, to be alone, to deepen its identity and its intimacy with God; but there is also a time to open wide the doors.

Hospitality is a way of life that is due for a comeback. It is the smile that greets friend and stranger. It is the warm embrace, and the welcome of each person as a gift from God.

Human and healing

God made us human beings, not human doings.
Robert Warren

In the film *Dances with Wolves* the Native American Chief Kicking Bear says to a US Army Chief, 'Of all the trails in life there is one that matters more than all the others. It is the trail of the true human being.' How many of our churches are on that trail?

'What does it mean to be fully human?' Here are some answers I have received to this question:

to be real
to make good relationships
to be a good lover
to be sensual, understanding, and beautiful inside
to be in touch with your feelings
to flow in your potential
to have masculine-feminine balance
to be healthy in mind and body
to be free
to live and die well
to appreciate good food, friends and things
to appreciate the wonder of life
being alive with all your senses
to be deep but full of fun.

An Indian elder (Oriah Medicine Dreamer) put it this way:

> I want to know if you will risk looking like a fool for love, for your dream, for the adventure of being alive . . . I want to know if you have touched the centre of your own sorrow, if you have been opened by life's betrayals or have become shrivelled and closed by fear of further pain! I want to know if you can sit down with pain, mine or your own, without moving to hide or fade it or fix it. I want to know if you can be with JOY, mine or your own, if you can dance with wildness or let the ecstasy fill you to the tips of your fingers and toes. I want to know if you can disappoint another to be true to yourself, if you can bear the accusation of betrayal and not betray your own soul. I want to know if you can see beauty even when it is not pretty every day and if you can source your life on the edge of the lake and shout to the silver of the full moon, YES!!

How can churches enable us to become more fully human?

First, by grasping the biblical rationale for this. The reason a church should seek to be fully human is that our humanness is what reflects God's likeness in us. The glory of God is seen in a human life – its sensuality, intellect, relationships, work, creativity and worship lived to the full. To be fully human is to tie in with our original intention. To be redeemed is to be redeemed into all that we are meant to be; to be like Jesus, who is the most complete human being.

Second, by distinguishing between good and evil. By creating humans in the divine image, God endowed us with an innate capacity for doing this. We can distinguish between good and evil by following an inner law that arouses the emotions appropriate to each: shame, fear, guilt are signs we're making wrong choices. Joy, resolution and confidence are signs we are making right choices. It is this innate capacity to distinguish between good and evil which we inherit from Adam. It is not Adam's sexual acts, but his example in making wrong choices, which turns us from good to evil.

Third, by revitalising the concept of Mother Church. There is an old Hebridean saying: 'There is a mother's heart in the heart of God.' For the last decade of his life the Scotsman William Sharpe (1855-1905) wrote under the pseudonym of Fiona Macleod, perhaps thus reconnecting with his more feminine self. In his book *Iona*, published in 1910 he recalls this old Celtic prophecy:

> The Holy Spirit shall come again . . . All will be aware of the descending of the Divine Womanhood upon the human heart as a universal spirit descending upon waiting souls.

Prophecy needs to be tested, and not all that comes from Macleod's pen passes that test, but perhaps this prophecy does.

Robert Warren, when he was the Church of England's Evangelism Officer, reminded many congregations that 'churches should become the places, par excellence, where the general public can find out how to live fully human lives.' A lady told me, 'I don't want to go to a church that will judge me, but to one that will understand me.' She will find a home in churches that reflect the mother heart of God.

A former Elim pastor named Mark was reading Robert Warren's book *Being Human: Being Church*. He was now minister of a small independent fellowship. 'How do we become a fully human church?' he asked.

We broke this huge challenge into four areas:
1) Clear thinking about what it means from God's point of view (theology);

2) Dismantling frameworks that inhibit this;
3) Developing a lifestyle that expresses it;
4) Dealing with pitfalls that undermine it.

As Mark and I began discussing how a church can become human he kept interjecting, 'But our members would not go along with that.' For example, they might assume that the way to move into God's presence is 1980s-style celebration; so to have a time of worship in which there was no such singing or prophecy would be unthinkable. A stylised frame had replaced being real together before God. So, first, his church had to dismantle a particular style, which members associated with being fully Spirit-filled. Or they might plan a social occasion to which the public were invited, but because members felt driven to corner each non-Christian and ask them to receive Jesus, the relish of the occasion and the spontaneity of friendship was lost. It became unnatural, and the guests never came again. So the stylised framework of evangelism had to be dismantled. His members had to be taught that Jesus built a relationship with people before he asked them to follow him.

Mark believes that a church of people who are becoming fully human connects with people at many places and levels, whereas old-style approaches disconnect them. Thus his church hosts a harvest service that honours local businesses and education centres.

Households

> We have taken the major events of the home like birth, marriage and death, and have anaesthetised them by placing them in church.
>
> *Archdeacon Martin Wallace*

At first sight no two things have less in common than home life in biblical times and home life today. A Jewish or Celtic home was a long-established, extended household around which the basic things of life revolved. A modern family has been described as a temporary arrangement of beds around a fridge and a microwave oven; the important things happen elsewhere. Yet there is a golden thread that links the two: as the sparrow yearns to build a nest so does the human being.

Jewish and Celtic models of the church in the home can spur modern Christians to exchange artificial churchy duties for that of enjoying God together in their homes.

The Christianity of the Celts was a spirituality of the hearth before it was a spirituality of the church. Every household chore became a liturgy, because they practised ritually being present to God in each thing that they did. Thus familiar prayers for lighting the fire, dressing, cleaning, cooking, eating, welcoming visitors, retiring to bed, became second nature. Births, marriages, deaths, anniversaries, home-comings were all celebrated in the home.

Contemporary household rituals are being well used. See, for example, Volume Three of *The Celtic Prayer Book*.[4] In some circles it is becoming fashionable to create prayer corners in homes. A study, workroom, eating room or bedroom may nowadays merge into an area of icons, candles, prayer cards, Bibles or tokens of creation that evoke adoration.

I believe many churches should release people from churchy duties which they are not really called to, and encourage these practices:

1. A weekly meal in households. During these each person is present to those who wish to tell of their 'journey' that week. A candle is lit and prayer is offered. Friends who have no such household are invited to join them. A

4. *The Celtic Prayer Book,* Volume Three, *Healing the land: sacraments and special services* (Kevin Mayhew 2003).

spare place is laid for Christ in the guise of the stranger or the unseen guest. This may take the form of the Jewish Shabat meal on Friday evenings, which Christians increasingly use.

2. A yearly blessing of the home with a celebration. Some people do this on St Brigid's Day, 1 February, and combine it with the custom of placing a Brigid Cross made of rushes in the home and extending this to storerooms, outhouses, caravans, boats which have been disused during the season of dark. Congregations who have adopted the cell model have a head start, but it is important that every member's home, where permission is given, is visited and blessed once a year.

Mystical and connected to the unseen world

I am deeply convinced that great renewal will develop wherever communities enter regularly into solitude. Time for silence, individual study, personal prayer and meditation must be seen to be as important to all the members of the community as working together, playing together and worshipping together. Without solitude we cannot experience each other as different manifestations of a love that transcends us all.

Henri Nouwen

'The biggest problem with evangelical Christianity,' an evangelical pastor told me, 'is that they have to know all the answers. It robs them of so much.' Emerging churches foster windows of the soul, that is, the ability to read the signs of God's life in our everyday and inner worlds. This is spiritual literacy, heart knowledge, a way of awareness and seeing. *Spiritual Literacy: Reading the Sacred in Everyday Life* provides a stimulating anthology on this theme.[5]

5. Brussat, Frederic and Mary Ann *Spiritual Literacy: Reading the Sacred in Everyday Life* (Simon & Schuster, 1998).

In his letter to the church of Laodicea (Revelation 3) John urges the value of purity (white) and of inner seeing – churches need people whose eyes are washed in continual contemplation. Things that prevent this way of seeing in congregations are a world-view that dismisses mystical and personal experience as worthless.

The deep need in the human soul for divine contemplation has long been repressed, but is now making itself felt. There is a mushrooming of prayer cells and *poustinias* in houses, gardens and monasteries. as well as of prayer corners.

How do church members who discover they are called to contemplative prayer stay in their church if it has no place for it? The vision of a cradle-in-the-making needs to be shared with their churches. Cradles are different from organisations.

> The greatest challenge to the church in the third millennium is to relate in a Christ-centred way to the Unseen World, which people on the Alternative scene are far more at home with than are Christians.
>
> *James Turnbull*

Many of the most spiritual people believe in, visualise or encounter spiritual beings. Yet Protestantism has said that the things of heaven are unknowable. Second-millennium churches tended to ignore the biblical model of the Divine Assembly. The writer of the Book of Job depicts the Almighty as presiding over an assembly of Divine offspring, (Job 6). The second verse of the Bible in Hebrew speaks of 'the Spirit Elohim' covering the face of the earth. Exodus 19 describes Moses going up to the Mount of the Elohim where one of the Elohim spoke to him. El-lohim is a feminine word (El) with a masculine plural. It means 'the divine beings or powers' at work in the human or in the otherworld. The offspring of El were still active in New Testament days; for example Gabri-El (strength of El), Micha-El (likeness of El). At Jesus' birth the angels praised El and Jesus is described as the Son of El, (Immanu-El, Matthew 1:23).

The Bible also names God as the Most High. This makes us aware that there is a hierarchy of beings, at the summit of which is the Most High. Another biblical name for God is the Lord of Hosts. There were a host of beings, earthly and heavenly, which constituted this host.

There are polarities within God: male and female (Genesis 1:27), light and darkness (Isaiah 45:7); Yahweh is both a warrior and a mother (Isaiah 42:13,14).

Ezekiel saw a vision of Yahweh in the form of four living creatures representing the four fixed signs of Taurus, Aquarius, Leo and Scorpio. Both models reappear in the last book of the Bible, the Apocalypse of St John, in the seven spirits of El Elyon and the four living creatures surrounding the throne of the Lamb (i.e. Christ, Rev. 4:6). No aspect of creation is left out of the Divine Assembly. The cosmos was a unified organism, a macrocosm, which is reflected in each individual who is a microcosm. There were planetary deities. Using a system that united the seven known planets of the day with the characteristics of the zodiacal signs, the Sumerians had worked out the general patterns involved in each individual life. That need not detract from the freedom that is the birthright of each human being, and which Christ came to give back to us. To this day the motto of genuine astrology remains 'The stars dispose but they do not determine'.

If gods and goddesses are seen for what they are, symbolic representations of created powers and energies, the raw material of cosmic life in all its diverse aspects, then they need to be valued in the light of their motivation. Often, in the Old Testament, prophets called believers to renounce false or evil gods; this was because they were in opposition to the Most High. In other passages God's spokesperson calls on the beings to bow down to the Most High, but not to disappear. The Greek version of Deuteronomy 32:43 bears this out:

Rejoice with him, O heavens
Bow down to him sons of God [i.e. Elohim, sons of El]
Rejoice with his people, nations
Confirm him, all you angels of God.

Relationship and soul friends

'See how these Christians love one another' was a common saying in the first few centuries of the church. Since those times, those who wish to become members of the church have been required to accept a creed which states what they are to believe, but they have not been required to accept the Beatitudes (the beautiful attitudes commended by Jesus, Matthew 5:1-12), which state how they are to relate. The emerging church puts the Beatitudes on a level with the creeds.

If the loving church is to replace the judgemental church, cells within the Body of Christ will have to learn new conditioned reflexes. Members of churches who visit Lindisfarne often ask, 'How do we bring this about?' They want to serve Jesus, but do not want to do this in churches that are dominated by committees, clerics and conventions. I advise them to exercise faith. That is, to act as if relationship is primary in every conversation, committee and circumstance.

One church encourages any member who had upset another to take them a love gift the following day.

Equality of regard has become an accepted principle in our society. It was, for example, a building block of the

1998 Northern Ireland Good Friday Agreement. The emerging church has to be a community where this principle is practised.

At the heart of the doctrine of God is a communion of loving selves. In a book entitled *Trinity for Atheists* Italian theologian Bruno Forte describes the Trinity as 'a communion of flowing relationships'. We can only find our true identity as persons by reflecting this communion. As Charles Williams observed: it is as important to learn how we live *from* each other as how we are to live *for* each other.

In St Aidan's ancient kingdom of Northumbria there are still people, like him, who model church as friendship. When Revd Catherine Hooper, who had parishes in the Gateshead area, was killed in a car crash in 1999 a neighbour told the *Daily Telegraph*: 'It took her ages to walk to church because she was stopped by so many people along the way who wanted to talk to her. Before she came here very few people came to the church, but afterwards it was always packed, especially with young people.' [6]

People-friendly

True evangelism always happens from within the culture. To adopt a new faith does not imply adopting a new culture.
Martin Wallace

The Christian faith never exists except as 'translated' into culture.
David Bosch [7]

6. *Daily Telegraph*, 29 May 1999.

7. Bosch, David J. *Transforming Mission: Paradigm Shifts in Theology of Mission* (Maryknoll, New York, Orbis Books, 1991).

In the 1990s John Finney conducted research for the United Bible Societies in Britain on how people find faith. He summarised the findings in four words: 'Belonging comes before believing.' In the USA George Hunter's research led him to a similar conclusion: More and more of the converts he questioned had felt that they were included and wanted in the church before they believed. [8]

Second-millennium churches often thought it was necessary to crush all pre- and non-Christian spirituality for the sake of Jesus. It is true that if the church surrenders its soul to the spirit of the age it will have nothing to give, but it is equally true that if it fails to enter the soul of the people it will fail to give what it has. The Christian community has to be distinct from culture and yet immersed in it, as Jesus showed us.

Jesus was able to become one with the people in all things except sin because he remained one with the divine Spirit. That enabled him to lose earthly power, and become king of human hearts.

His critics, the Pharisees, had big evangelistic campaigns, but failed to turn round the hearts of the people. They imposed their culture, whereas Jesus stroked the people's culture. He took prime time to involve himself in their typical social gatherings (for example a wedding at Cana, John 2), religious gatherings (at synagogues) and occupations (for example, fishing). He gave himself to the poor, and did not put extra burdens upon them. He went to the most popular event of the year (Pentecost Festival Holiday) and illustrated his message with the most universally valued commodity – water. When Jesus made water taste like

8. Hunter, George *The Celtic Way of Evangelism*, p. 54 (Abingdon Press, USA, 1999).

good wine (John 2) the need being met was a neighbour-hood celebration whose swing was threatened – an extended family whose good name for hospitality was in the balance.

Some churches hedge round the Christian message as something 'unregenerate' people cannot understand. Jesus believed in freedom of information for all people. He held 'talkathons' in large open-air auditoriums (e.g. Matthew 5-7).

In order to baptise our culture we have to see it from the inside as God does. What is of God in it? How is God present in it? [9]

Emerging churches face the people. When someone took pot shots at one of her convents in a new York slum area Mother Teresa quietly went into the backyard, a tiny square of rubble and clothes lines, with an old, peeling statue of Mary, which faced the sisters while they worked in the kitchen. Mother Teresa stood there for a few minutes and then said, 'Turn the statue around. Let her face the people.' The sisters were never shot at again. [10]

This story is a parable for each church to apply in its own way. One church in a large Leeds housing estate began to face the people when its Bingo club, which was losing members, asked the vicar if she would come and bless it. She offered to extend the blessing into a service. They were so thrilled with this that they asked if they could have a regular service. This became known as the Bingo church.

Emerging churches 'befriend the chiefs'. The first evangel-ists in the British Isles had to persuade local rulers to open doors to them before any mission could begin. Post-modern society is becoming 'tribal' again and the church must

9. Shorter, Aylward *Evangelisation and Culture* (Chapman, 1994).

10. *The Plough* October 1997.

learn to relate to the different people groups. A bishop advised a new young priest to 'target the tribal chiefs' in his local housing estate. The police had lost control there, and a local mafia, who cruised the estate in expensive cars financed from drugs, took charge. They had a code, which meant that they 'looked after' the local community. When the vicarage was twice vandalised the new minister informed the local newspaper that he cared about the local community and was too poor to own the church house he lived in. On reading this, the leader of the 'mafia' befriended the vicar, and promised to protect him and provide for the community. The 'mafia' provided a superb community fireworks display with cans of beer aplenty. The debilitating cycle of dependency, which marked other estates where the council ran everything, was being broken; a community was being empowered in certain ways.

Emerging churches start from where local residents are. They follow the principle 'Do not try to teach anyone anything until you have learnt something from them.' If we start where people are, we will find that most people, even though they are unchurched, have a bank of spiritual experience upon which we may draw. God can and does speak to human beings because they are human beings, not because they are Christians. The Bible records many examples of this, none of which denies the necessity for witness.

The Alister Hardy Research Unit has discovered that nearly two thirds of the British population admit to having religious experiences, but that for a number of reasons people rarely talk about them. This includes children. Researchers such as David Hay [11] and Rebecca Nye conclude that for all children, not just those who have been taught

11. Hay, D. *Religious Experience Today* (Mowbray/Cassell, 1990).

religious beliefs, spirituality is an essential aspect of life.[12] They uncover three categories of spiritual sensitivity in children which they call awareness sensing, mystery sensing and value sensing. These make possible the exploration of spirituality in a broader context than the traditionally recognised languages. Their findings suggest that children's natural 'relational consciousness' has been distorted or repressed by false constructs of Christianity. 'Value blockage' in Christian culture has been caused by factors which include the adoption of the imperial mode by the church, which became an instrument of control; the assimilation by the church of dualistic Greek ideas; and the abdication by seventeenth-century theologians from defending spiritual awareness as a valid source of knowledge.[13]

My friend Liz Cannon, whose paper 'Children's Spirituality – an Unexpected Store' contributed to this research, asks: 'Could it be that our secular culture is crushing the spirituality which is natural to children? Is it that at some level they discern that to be accepted in the secular culture of today, they have to let go of something which is very much part of them and integral to their life and wellbeing? And this crushing of children's natural integrated spirituality . . . even contributes to certain children's behaviour problems?' Retreating churches feared open exploration of spirituality, they exercised power by telling children what they 'ought' to hear rather than discovering God 'from whom every family on earth takes its name' (Ephesians 3:15).

12. Nye, R. and Hay, D. 'Investigating Children's Spirituality: How Do You Start Without a Starting Point?' *British Journal of Education* 18:3.

13. Nye, R. and Hay, D. 'Investigating Children's Spirituality: How Do You Start Without a Starting Point?' *British Journal of Education* 18:3, p. 152.

Mike Pilavachi is an Anglican who has started the Soul Survivor church near Watford. He likens the traditional Anglican Church, which he says he loves, to a high-class French restaurant whose cuisine and menu is entirely French. He likens churches such as Soul Survivor to McDonalds – cheap, cheerful and accessible – where most of the population feel more at home. The church grew out of Mike's passion for 'just doing church without the religious stuff'. When he is challenged about colluding with anti-Christian culture he answers: 'There are aspects of all cultures that are unchristian . . . the question is, can cultures be redeemed? Jesus was part of his culture and was counter-cultural to some aspects of it.'[14]

Earth-friendly

Christ's work is the ultimate reconciliation of all living creatures.

Karl Barth (commentary on Colossians 1)

'My church teaches me to be reconciled with God and with people, but it does not teach me to be reconciled to the earth,' Catherine informed me. That could be said of most second-millennium churches.

Many people seek a spirituality that is natural, and they feel violated if the church puts on unnatural airs, or neglects the earth.

Conservative twentieth-century churches rebuked those who claimed to find God in a garden. 'That is nature religion. It needs no Saviour,' they said. The result was that people like William Hague, Britain's 1990s Conservative leader, declared that they went to church one Sunday a month, walked in the countryside the other Sundays, and gained more benefit from the latter.

14. Interview in *Celebrate*, Friday, 3 December 1999.

Our pre-Christian forebears instinctively understood that the marriage of the human population with the fertile soil is necessary to the well-being of both. In the early myths of the Celts the god of the tribe mates with the goddess of the earth.[15] In the light of Christian revelation and modern science that instinct may be seen as at heart sound. The early Church, secure in its Jewish roots, understood this. God named the first man Earth (Adamah). Mr Earth's first act was to name, and thereby bless, each of earth's creatures (Genesis 2:20). In other words, the human being contains within itself the whole earth. Jesus Christ, who St Paul names 'the second Adam' (1 Corinthians 15:47) comes from heaven, yet contains within his humanity the whole evolving earth story, and its groaning in anticipation of its coming total fulfilment (Romans 8:19-23).

Several centuries passed. Augustine taught that creation was an act of God's power. Celtic Christians saw that creation was an act of God's love. Maximus the Confessor (d. 662) taught that the Creator-Logos has implanted in each created thing a characteristic 'thought', which is God's presence in and intention for it; this is its inner essence, which makes it distinctively itself and at the same time draws it towards God. By virtue of this indwelling logos each created thing is not just an object but a personal word addressed to us by the Creator. Thus the second Person of the Trinity acts as an all-embracing and unifying cosmic Presence.

The Celtic churches understood Christ, and therefore his Body, the Church, as 'the bough' of creation. This way

15. Sjoestedt, Marie-Louise *Gods and Heroes of the Celts* (Berkeley, Turtle Island Foundation, 1982).

of seeing the creation drained away when bureaucratic ways came to dominate the minds and machinery of the Church.

The emerging church grasps this cosmic fullness of Jesus. It opens its doors to the whole earth community. The hundreds of thousands of people who follow the 'word' God has put within them to cherish the earth, but do not know the story or the home of this 'word', will at last realise that creation is safe with Christians, and they will come home.

Earth, as a result of human action, is experiencing a monumental change. God is speaking to us through this. Our generation has been chosen by God to respond to the most momentous period of change in the billions of years of earth's history. The chemistry, bio-systems, geology and ozone layer are changing more radically than ever they have, and life systems are being extinguished at an unparalleled rate.

Creative arts

The emerging church walks hand in hand with the creative arts, because human creativity is a reflection of the Creator, though it must always cater for non-artistic people who value order more than experiment. The churches that have survived best provide a predictable framework, which includes treasured, unchanging words and creeds, but they use these as a springboard for creativity, not as a straitjacket.

When Kim Erickson Haire worked as a waitress in various American cities, she became aware of a large group of people who were quite different from the people she met in churches. She calls these 'the fluid people'. Fluid people, she observes, congregate at the vegetarian restaurant during Sunday lunch, while 'the Christians are institutionalised, singing words which originate on the surface of a page, skim the surface of their hearts, and echo off the surface of church walls.' She continues:

Fluid people are liquid; they are poured into life and moving with the tide of the cosmos. They pour their spirits into art. Their souls feel somehow connected to the movement of the earth, and they search for meaning through colour, movement and harmony.

Maybe the nerves somehow transfer differently to the brain, for this person actually feels colour; he flows with the shades, the depth and the richness; he becomes a part of its movement without form. She sees music, not as notes on a page, but as sounds which form movement in mirrors of light in her imagination, and if she is a praying person, she prays a dance to her God. He hears a rhythm that needs no music, it is the music of the earth, the strum of the wind, the gasp of the waves, the pulses of nature. She tastes the pain, the bitterness in the depth of a heart, or the sweetness which waits eagerly in the soul. He smells hope like expectant snow, clean and fresh; hope ready to burst through the cold greyness with brilliant crystals reflecting the true light of heaven . . .

Kim Haire concludes that most fluid people are consumed with the spiritual world, but few relate to Christ. She believes that the icon can be a powerful tool for discipling the fluid person. 'The icon,' she writes, 'has an intrigue which arouses the imagination and stimulates the senses of a person . . . it does not bend to the theatrical; it does not flaunt a gaudy Jesus on black velvet . . . The icon reaches mysteriously from the cosmic realm into the human realm . . . To a believer, this truth is Christ – to the unbeliever it is a mystery, a mystery calling, urging, drawing the lost to seek and enter the kingdom of God.' [16]

It is important that churches do not let the arts they use be divorced from the ever-fresh wells of creativity. In the stillness of dawn, fresh springs come to light.

16. Notes supplied by John Smith from his seminary in USA.

The retreating Church's neglect of the poetry in people created a vacuum, which, here and there, other groups have tried to fill. For example, Ian McMillan has been employed as poet-in-residence of both Barnsley Football Club and Northern Spirit train company in West Yorkshire. [17] Peter Sanson, the poet hired by Marks and Spencer to bring out 'the creative side' of its 57,000 employees, believes that everyone has a poet inside them. [18]

Poets were part of the birthright of the biblical church.

> The true poet is really a prophet. His gaze looks on things that others miss. It is no accident that in the original manuscripts, the words of the Old Testament prophets were written in poetic form.
>
> *Denny Gunnerson*

The Welsh poet and archbishop of Canterbury, Rowan Williams, describes the work of the poet as 'interpreting and harmonising the flow of the world's life in such a way that the shifts and changes of the world . . . can be unveiled as transfiguration, epiphanies of God's life.' [19]

Emerging churches weave poetry into their worship, and the larger ones appoint bards.

Poetry leaves some people cold, and churches should be places where non-poetic people feel at home. These often respond to the good telling of a story. My journalist friend, Clive Price, met a member of a church in Denver, Colorado, which was founded by American Indians. Clive told him what went on at a typical church meeting in Britain. 'Oh, we don't do anything like that,' the church member

17. *The Times* 15 July 1999.
18. *The Week* 13 December 1997.
19. Williams, Rowan *Ffydd ac Argyfwng Cenedl (Faith and the Crisis of a Nation) Vol. 2* (John Penri Press, Swansea, 1982).

replied, 'when we gather together we spend the time telling stories.'[20]

The retreating church either idolised or rejected signs and symbols. The emerging church, reflecting Christ's ministry, which overflowed with living symbols, celebrates the glory of God in painting and poetry, colour and sound, movement and music, symbol and drama. It brings colour back into the streets; it uses oil, water, fire, the earth and all its fruits. It seeks to rekindle a Christian imagination.

Roger Ellis of Revelation Church, Sussex, is giving himself to a church, which is, in his words, emerging from the culture, not insulting it. He and Chris Seaton describe in their book, *The New Celts*, how God is leading them to establish culture-friendly café churches for young people, and to use creative arts in worship:

> We have encouraged artists to come and draw what they feel is happening as the church worships together. We have also had sculptors and even potters working to one side of the meeting. Sometimes, in the process of the worship the artists are encouraged to interpret what it is they are portraying. At other times the work is left to stand in its own right and people are invited to go and view it at the end and ask the Holy Spirit to speak to them. [21]

In his book, *Which Way for the Church?*, [22] the Revd Dr Rob Frost foresees a vital role for the arts in the Church of the new millennium:

> Music will take greater prominence and will become integral to the prayer experience. Prayer through music will be

20. Indian Bible Church, 595 South Logan Street, Denver, Colorado 80209 USA.
21. Ellis, Roger and Seaton, Chris *New Celts* (Kingsway Publications, 1998).
22. Frost, Rob *Which Way for the Church?* (Kingsway Publications, 1996).

commonplace, be it sung Evensong, jazz mass, folk celebration or classic meditation.

The new churches will rediscover art, from the iconography of the East to the statues of Rome, and they will develop their own contemporary spirituality through it. Frequently changing displays, pictures, posters and banners will become a growing inspiration for prayer as the churches learn how to use the visual arts as a means and not an end . . .

In the new church, drama will be seen as a prime means of effective communication. Actor Nigel Forde wrote 'Prophetic theatre is theatre which clarifies the word of God at a particular time; Evangelistic theatre is that which clarifies the gospel in particular; Didactic theatre – in this context – clarifies the teaching of the Bible, and Entertaining theatre is based on the nature of human kind and creation . . .'

The arts will not change or cheapen the gospel, nor will they replace preaching; they will complement it. The language of film, music, drama, poetry and dance will be the vernacular of the new generation, and the church will learn how to speak it, and speak it fluently.

Unity and justice

During the second millennium three great strands of Christianity became separated: the catholic strand of community around the Real Presence of Christ in the Eucharist; the Protestant strand of personal conversion around the Bible; and the Orthodox (and in a sense the Pentecostal) strand of worship around an experience of the Holy Spirit. It was laid upon me that God wanted to weave these three strands together again, and that we were to let him weave them together in us as he willed.

Jesus said to his apostles, 'Whoever listens to you, listens to me.' The apostles were not always right, but they had been selected, they had responded, they spent time with Jesus. So we have to make an act of unity with the original apostles. I journeyed to the tombs in Rome in order to make an act of unity with Peter (a symbol of the Roman Catholic churches), with Paul (a symbol of Protestant churches, since he rebuked Peter for wrong behaviour), and I have subsequently made an act of unity with John (a symbol of the churches in Eastern and Celtic lands).

In his autobiographical book *Conjectures of a Guilty Bystander* (1966) Thomas Merton wrote: 'If I can unite in myself the thought and devotion of Eastern and Western Christendom, the Greek and the Latin Fathers, the Russian with the Spanish Mystics, I can prepare in myself the reunion of divided Christians . . . If we want to bring together what is divided we cannot do so by imposing one division upon another or absorbing one tradition into another. We must contain all the divided worlds in ourselves and transcend them in Christ.' In some deep and mysterious way, God was speaking also to me along these lines.

We have to make an act of unity with those God has placed in oversight in the churches today. There is disagreement as to how these leaders are meant to be appointed, but we all need to see that God has provided for our unity by giving us leaders. We should honour those who have been placed in oversight over churches that follow the orthodox Christian Faith. This need not mean blind obedience – which in our plural society could not be the custom. But neither does it mean that everyone does what is right in their own eyes. It means each of us should listen carefully, weigh thoughtfully, and communicate respectfully to other overseers.

Then we have to make an act of unity with God's Word in the Bible. Although Christians may have different understandings of the Bible, every Christian is required to approach it with deep humility, hungry to be fed, as a lover eagerly poring over a love letter from their beloved.

We have to make an act of unity with Jesus in Holy Communion. This sacrament means just that, Christians communing together with their Lord, visibly. Every time we receive the bread and wine we should make ourselves one with the whole Body of Christ on earth and in heaven. Certain sections of the world church ban baptised members of other churches from receiving the bread and wine. This is on the grounds that they have broken away from the one church, and have therefore broken the biblical conditions for receiving Communion. Those who are excluded should adopt the attitude of the foreign woman who begged Jesus to give her some food, even if only the scraps left for the dog. Don't stay away, beg for scraps, which can take various forms according to local inspirations. Many churches, however, have an open table – it is open to all the beggars of the world who are hungry to be fed by Jesus. These open tables become powerful signs and experiences of unity, and emerging churches will have the spirit of the open table.

CHAPTER 6

The Challenges to the
Main Church Streams

All the Church streams face fundamental challenges. This chapter explores some of them and how Churches are facing up to them.

The Church of England

Five tasks confront the Church of England.

1. To move from the diocesan to a modern monastic system.

2. To engender a homogeneous body of believers.

3. To turn the 'Comprehensive Church' into the 'Church of Hospitality'.

4. To develop worship that is a vehicle for the people's best aspirations.

5. To release a new generation of leaders from the old straitjackets.

The main thrust of central church planning in the last decade of the century was how to decline efficiently.

Attempts were made to prop up the old system. Parishes were amalgamated and empty vicarages were filled with non-stipendiary ministers. Some diocesan leaders, however have begun to recognise that a historic change is taking place, and that more is needed.

The second task of engendering homogeneity is formidable. Many young as well as old clergy think of themselves as 'evangelicals', 'Reform', 'Catholics', 'Forward in Faith', 'liberals', 'post-evangelicals' or 'charismatics' first, as Anglicans second and as members of the Christian church third. It is the disease that Paul warned against: 'When some of you say, "I belong to Paul's group" and others say, "I belong to Apollos' group" don't you realise you are behaving like non-Christians?' (1 Corinthians 3:4).

The Church of England has talked much about its role as a 'Comprehensive' church. This led many to believe that it stood for anything or nothing. Yet within this concept is a God-given seed, deep in the soul of the nation, which now needs to be planted out in the sunlit topsoil. This seed is Hospitality. Hospitality can bind all sections of the church in a common vision. It means welcoming all people as they are, until they feel able to bring their needs to the church and to its God. It means not putting upon them alien requirements, but providing welcoming space and an affirming presence in which they may journey.

Anglicans have a reputation for cultural aloofness and elitism. They are prone to despise other ways, which they think lack aesthetic excellence, such as happy clappy Pentecostal worship, or ethnic bands. Outsiders can find Anglican ways introverted, lukewarm, incomprehensible and inhospitable. To encourage the life of God in those of different cultures, to release them and give them opportunity – that is hospitality. To make space for groups, so that they find and embrace the true and eternal love – that is what it means to be a comprehensive church.

The way the Church of England handled the funeral of Princess Diana gave us a glimpse of how it might tackle the fourth task, of expanding its worship until it becomes a vehicle of the people's aspirations. Such expansion is vital. A vicar of a community-based church in an urban priority area told me he could not use the Church of England's prescribed forms of worship: they were a joke at local level. He could use the Iona Community's Wild Goose worship resources, because of their lack of wordiness, their down to earth imagery and the worth they give to people. (The four-volume *Celtic Prayer Book* compiled by the author is a recent contribution to this needed transformation.)

The fifth task, to release a new generation of leaders at every level, is being tackled only patchily. Recently management criteria have been applied in the selection of ordinands. It was certainly long overdue that clergy be trained in management skills. But it is possible to be a good leader or a good pastor without being a good manager, and managers are being ordained who have skin-deep spirituality.

The Church of England threw out abuses at the Reformation, but kept bishops, even though medieval bishops abused their powers. This did not lead to wholesale prelature because the church also kept 'the parson's freehold'. This meant that a patron (who might be a local landowner or an organisation founded to maintain certain beliefs) could appoint a vicar or rector to a parish who would then have a legal right to that post, and the house that went with the post, until they resigned or retired. A bishop could not sack the parson except for gross misconduct or heresy.

This system had patent faults. But what has replaced it? The sausage machine. The non-freehold system prevents lame ducks from being forever given a sinecure, but it also prevents saints, prophets or other Christians who are called to be pastors from offering unconditional love. For you don't move on after a temporary contract expires if you really love people. Many priests are now required to move after a short term.

Much better to replace this with a compulsory review with the bishop every seven years or so.

> Whenever I see a bishop in dispute with a parish it is because the parish wants to grow but bishops are planning for long-term decline.
>
> *A cathedral vice-dean*

The most telling leadership in the Church of England has come from people such as the leaders of New Wine movements and Alpha courses. These are evidence that strong leadership is possible in today's church.

The Anglican (Episcopal) Communion

Two and a half million French-speaking Africans in the Congo are Anglicans, yet their church was founded by fellow African missionaries and songs freshly composed by members are used every time they worship. The Anglican Communion has mushroomed across the five continents. In its early days, the consensus was that it should see itself as provisional, and aim to merge with a reformed catholic church. That view is no longer dominant. For it models a form of church in which each province is autonomous, but the bishops are bound together in common bonds of belief, worship and history, which provides a norm for the future.

If this Communion is meant by God to be one of the major continuing strands in the cord which is being rewoven, then it must surely change its name from Anglican to Episcopal Communion. Why? A stream of Christ's Church which claims to be worldwide and contiguous with the original Church is foolish to define itself in terms of an ethnic group (Angles), even if a particular ethnic group played a significant part in shaping its structures. The Scottish Episcopal Church and the USA Episcopal Church eschewed the colonial overtones of the title 'Anglican'. If the Anglican Communion views itself as a parallel, in the West, to the Orthodox Church in the East, it might well start to parallel the Orthodox style of terminology. Thus we would have the English Episcopal Church, the Papua New Guinea Episcopal Church, and the Japanese Episcopal Church, each in communion with the Archbishop of Canterbury. Just as Byzantium became a second Rome in the first millennium, there might be a new Canterbury before the end of the third millennium, situated in Africa or Asia. The Archbishop of this Canterbury, like the Patriarchs of the Orthodox Church, will probably by then be in communion with the Bishop of Rome.

The Orthodox

The composer, John Tavener, whose *Song for Athene* touched so many people at the funeral of Diana, Princess of Wales in September 1997, was brought up in the Presbyterian church but converted to Orthodoxy when he was 30. Ruth Gledhill of *The Times* interviewed him after his return from the funeral of an old Orthodox woman. 'It was so tender, so personal, everyone standing around the open coffin with candles, with no pomp, no ceremony,' he told her. He could understand why so many were turning to Hinduism, Buddhism, Islam. 'There is an enormous humility there which does not seem to be present in the

Western church,' he told Gledhill. 'I can only see a future for Christianity if the whole world becomes Orthodox.' [1]

In the 1980s 2000 USA evangelicals were welcomed into the Orthodox Church, among them Peter Gillquist, a leader of Campus Crusade. They described Orthodoxy as 'America's Best Kept Secret'. The following decade both evangelical and catholic minded members of the Church of England joined Orthodox churches. In 1999 Ruth Gledhill wrote an article in *The Times* headed 'Goodbye Happy Clappers – Orthodox Christianity may pose a serious challenge to the mainstream churches.'

One American, an evangelical missionary in Rumania named David Hudson, wrote of his entry into Orthodoxy: 'Finally we got out of the stormy seas of pluralistic, idio-syncratic and eclectic Christianity and into the ark of the historic, original, continuing life of the Church.' [2] The Americans made Scripture memorisation, the Eucharist, familiar corporate prayers and silence their diet and met together daily at 6am. The Lord had spoken to them through the words of the prophet Jeremiah: 'Ask for the ancient paths, where the good road lies; walk in it and find rest for your souls' (Jeremiah 6:16). Michael Harper, a former curate at All Souls, Langham Place under John Stott, and the founder of the umbrella movement for Britain's early charismatic renewal, The Fountain Trust, is perhaps the most well known of the British converts. Why had he converted? He told me that, although the Orthodox Church had its own problems, it had avoided the split psyche

1. *The Times*, 13 September 1997.

2. Quoted in *Again*, Vol. 21 No. 2, April-June 1999, published by Conciliar Press, a department of the USA Antiochan Orthodox Christian Archdiocese.

that traumatised Reformed churches, and the Papalism which overlay the Roman Catholic Church. It maintained an organic continuity with the original New Testament Church.

A journal, *Orthodox England*, was launched in 1997 edited by Fr Andrew Phillips. Priests in the Church of England formed a movement named 'Journey Towards Orthodoxy'. Many of these, especially those who used to be part of the Anglo-Catholic movement, were looking for something to which they could belong. They, especially the 'J' personality types, needed clear identity, ethos, features and psycho-dynamics. They abhorred vagueness. They were ready to eschew legalism and formalism, but not for nothing. They wanted to be certain there was a kernel that was non-negotiable. That is why the Orthodox tradition appealed to them. The existence of this kernel frees them from the need to build an elaborate superstructure of rules and regulations. What is the kernel? The apostles, the Beatitudes, the Trinity, the prayer, the early church councils and the Fathers – God-breathed living tradition. An attractive feature of the ordained ex-Anglicans who become Orthodox is that they tend to set up centres of prayer in sheds! Stephen Weston, of Sutton, Norfolk designed and built his plywood construction; its formal name is St Fursey's Chapel, but its nickname is Stephen's Byzantine Shed!

The Orthodox throughout the world venerate the saints of the first millenium in every land and regard the church in Celtic lands in that period as the Orthodox Church. The glory of the Orthodox Church is its continuity, which its liturgies enshrine. It claims to be the only true church. However, it has little chance of becoming the 'People's Church' in Western lands unless it faces up to at least two challenges.

The first challenge is that many Eastern Orthodox Churches have become so culture-friendly that they are little more than the religious arm of nationalism, failing to combat dreadful atrocities in some lands and deep animosities towards fellow Orthodox and non-Orthodox in other lands. On the day in 1917 that ushered in 70 years of Communist tyranny in Russia, the Holy Synod of the Russian Orthodox Church was in conclave. Its agenda? The colour of vestments. It missed the revolution.

The second challenge is to Orthodox Churches in the West: By placing themselves under the jurisdiction of a patriarch from the Eastern Church, how can they claim to be the indigenous Church in the West?

The Celtic Orthodox Church has tried to address this. It sees itself as the Orthodox Church in Celtic lands (mainly Britain and France) and believes that its style and liturgy should therefore be indigenous. For this reason, although its bishop is in the apostolic succession and has been consecrated by a Syrian Orthodox patriarch, it will not place itself under the jurisdiction of a patriarch from the East. In their liturgy, unlike Eastern Orthodoxy, they allow people to see through the screen to the inner sanctuary in order to emphasise that the church is open to all and is not just for a select few priests. The heartbeat of the Celtic Orthodox Church is the monastery at St Dol, Brittany. Here six monks have lived holy lives for 20 years. In that time they have never purchased food; they rely for their food on what the people place in large baskets at each Sunday liturgy. These monks seek to build loving relationships with Catholics and others; and they reach out to young people, teaching them and accompanying their convoys of aid to stricken areas of Europe.[3] Other aspects of this

3. The Celtic Orthodox Church, Monastère Sainte-Presence, 56130 Saint-Dolay, France.

church, however, breathe the atmosphere of political machination.

A third challenge is that the Orthodox liturgy and church culture, which adherents claim to be original and essentially unalterable, does not, in fact, derive from the New Testament so much as from the time when the Roman Emperor Constantine made the Church the official religion of the Empire. God and the saints are cast in the imperial image. So when Orthodox Churches are founded in countries far removed from that empire in time and mentality, they are in fact alienating rather than saving institutions.

Did Orthodoxy stop doing theology creatively after the first seven Councils of the Church? Can it extricate itself from the imperial stream in which it was then swimming?

The Roman Catholic Church

Even before the Second Vatican Council, far-seeing Catholic theologians such as Nicholas Lash recognised that during the second millennium false forms of Roman Catholic consciousness had developed, such as the tendency to describe the Church as she now is, in language that is more properly reserved for the Church as she should be. Theo Westow points out that though Christ promised the gates of hell would never destroy the church, he never promised he would overrule perversion of its members. [4] So the institution, as well as individuals, can go wrong, as it did, says Westow, at the times of the great Orthodox Schism, the Crusades, the Reformation, and when it neglected the poor. He suggests that the Curia, which embodies

4. Westow, Theo *Introducing Contemporary Catholicism* (SCM Press Ltd, 1967).

wrong tendencies of the second millennium 'was in no sense instituted by Christ, has no theological foundation, has no theological authority.' Theo Westow, writing during good John XXIII's papacy, saw that two ways were open to his church: to stifle the corporate examination of conscience that John had begun, or to pursue it until Roman Catholicism is stripped of everything except Christ. To do this 'will mean that gradually we return to that "pilgrimage of the People of God", homeless, without security, creating the active presence of Christ in this world of brothers . . . It means that we recognise that we have rested long enough at the roadside, but that like the Jews on their journey through the desert, we must get up again and move.'

Westow foresaw that there had to be either repentance or judgement. In fact, there is both. The steep decline in membership and the crisis in the supply and well-being of priests is now chronic in the West, but there are also fresh approaches and new experiments in community.

A young leader of a vibrant new Roman Catholic community hopes to transplant similar communities near to ancient places of prayer. His family belong to the slender line of English people who refused to retract their obedience to the Pope at the time of England's break with Rome, even at the cost of having to worship in secret. 'I have one problem,' he told me, 'I do not feel English and most people don't treat Roman Catholics as truly English. Whatever I may think of the Anglican church, it has kept the Faith and spread it to the English people, whereas my church has a "minority mind-set".'

People who feel like this can make one of three responses. They can join the Church of England, remain Catholics with the defensive mind-set of a minority, or they can rekindle roots that are common to both the Church of England and the English Roman Catholic Church.

The late Basil Hume, Cardinal Archbishop of England and Wales at the end of the second millennium, broadcast his love of the Celtic saints, and modelled the life of a monk bishop. Roman Catholics in this tradition give to the Pope what belongs to his office as a successor to an apostle, but not what belongs to the local expression of the universal church.

Father Paul Dudziak of Maryland, USA is adopting this model, even though he thinks that as a priest of the Roman Catholic Church he starts from a disadvantaged position. He says of his church: 'Those who identify with the Reformation reject it as corrupt; those who identify with the Enlightenment reject it as ignorant; those who identify with Freudianism or Feminism reject it as oppressive. People in the West who are looking for spirituality turn East, because Western spirituality is inaccessible.' The challenge to his church, he believes, is to open the 'locked storehouse of western spirituality'.

New Churches

In the 1970s and 80s the New Churches were in front of the pack. They crossed fresh frontiers and took risks for God. Some of them had somewhat fallen back by the turn of the millennium, and were stuck in the mould of 20 years before. Sometimes they seemed less vulnerable, less open to the fresh horizons of the Spirit.

Ichthus churches maintained their original simplicity. They have refused, for example, to buy into buildings, and their pastors live most sparingly. They sustain relationships of trust with other sections of Christ's Church, and they faithfully seek to model Jesus' life in their corporate life.

Nevertheless, in the 1990s things that were lacking in this model came to the surface. The driving force of Ichthus was mission. Members and pastors were giving much but they were not receiving renewal in body-mind-spirit, either as individuals or as a community. They were not signs of the wholeness of God's kingdom. Members fell away, pastors became discouraged, congregations hived off.

Roger Forster, the founder, recognised that some things were not right. He shared his conviction that Ichthus had become too management dominated, and needed to rediscover its roots.

Des Figueredo is an Ichthus leader who pastors the Community Church in Balham, South London; he comes from a Goan Catholic background. A love for the people in his fellowship grew in him, and he felt God was calling him to be a father in God to his flock. This had implications. It meant, for example, that he himself had to say 'no' to some outside mission projects in order not to destroy the organic inner life of the local Body of Christ. His sense of call had other implications. Surely the local congregation is meant to be a community, not just a casual collection of transitory units? Could it be that the heart of the 'congregation' is more than the Sunday worship, the pastor and an office? Could those things revolve around a hub with a daily rhythm of prayer?

The Pioneer network of churches has sorted out certain crucial elements that make up true church: for example, community that is based on covenant (voluntary commitment to mutual relationship) rather than contract (which smacks of control). As new congregations are spawned and grow, the overall leaders are following a call to relinquish leadership of a congregation, and become mentors to those who take up that mantle. A former pagan eco-warrior who is now a member of a Pioneer church feels, however, that there are other equally important elements that have yet to be embraced such as rhythm, roots in wider Christianity and connectedness to the land.

New churches that have adopted Celtic-style features have been criticised for bolting on something to a framework, which fundamentally remains unchanged. Critics believe that the foundations need to become holistic, earth-friendly and catholic. One new church leader was heard to say, 'There is no room in our package for hermits.' Yet God has ways of getting dedicated Christians to make room.

A member of Rock Community Church, Dunbarton believes that people get attracted to community churches today as once they did to Celtic hermitages. 'Yet the use of liturgy in the Celtic style renewal frightens me. I came out of liturgical churches because they need to learn how to help people flow in the spirit,' he told me.

Members there meet in a school on Sundays. In their experience modern people can't all meet at one set time for corporate prayer, so they trust people to gather in groups when and where they feel. 'We've stopped being a hustle and bustle church . . .'

One question leaders of the new churches need to answer is: How do we recognise who is a true leader unless there is an external accreditation beyond their own community? Vineyard churches, reflecting their name, grew fast and naturally towards the end of last century. Their openness to the Holy Spirit, people and other churches, their creativity in worship and integrity in relationships, and their freedom from obsolete churchy culture, has proved to be a great blessing. John Wimber, their founder, who came out of the Jesus Movement of the 1970s, died in 1997. Vineyard churches now have to address some crucial issues. The first is: How do they relate at the deepest, organic level, to the universal body of Christ? The response to this issue of two North American Vineyard churches was to become part of the Orthodox Church. A Vineyard pastor known to me has transferred to a church within the apostolic succession because he came to believe that the sacraments and the ordained ministry were deeply connected with the continuity of Christ's church down the ages.

A second issue for Vineyard churches is how not to fossilise. Already some of them seem to be in a time warp of the previous generation, in worship and house style no longer relating to the culture around them, which has changed. Not every Vineyard pastor who has taken the risk of reaching across a new frontier has been supported.

Pentecostal Churches

A number of Pentecostal pastors have contacted us to explore how their churches can leave the old century behind and move on. I shall summarise their insights in the following imaginary introductory leaflet to One Way Pentecostal Church:

Welcome to One Way Pentecostal Church. We are the only church in this town that has the full gospel. Everyone here is baptised in the Spirit and speaks in tongues – which is the mark of every true believer.

Our worship is free from tradition and liturgy. Everyone speaks and praises God from their hearts – in tongues or in English – as the Spirit moves them.

We do not dress up in morbid clothes, and we praise God at all times – even at funerals.

We believe that if any one has faith they will be healed of sickness and their problems will disappear.

After the pastor discovered Celtic Renewal everything changed without anything having to be announced. He discovered the need to welcome God in tears as well as in tongues, in silence as well as in celebration. He realised that although they had glorified the Holy Spirit, they had ignored and therefore belittled the human spirit, which, because it is made in God's image, needs to be taken seriously.

Now he raises these challenges for his church: Do we have times for silence, for beauty, for sorrow? Do we recognise that we are vulnerable? Before, we could never relate to Jesus in the Garden of Gethsemane: can we now? Can we recognise other Christians as true brothers and sisters with whom we can share heart to heart, without writing them off as second-rate? Do we realise that the whole is greater than the parts?

Free Churches

Although the various Free Churches disagree about baptism, and about the degree of independence the local congregation should have, they share in common certain beliefs that came out of the sixteenth-century Reformation in Europe. These renounced the idea of a Christendom kept together by the Pope or by bishops in council, and espoused the idea of congregations whose authority lay in their members having a direct line to Christ through the Bible.

However, having transferred power from popes to church meetings, many ministers find that power has gone to the heads of church meetings quite as much as it ever did to the popes. 'I hardly know a Baptist minister in our region who has not had a breakdown,' one minister told me. Ministers are hired and fired by congregations, often on the basis of how many uncoordinated or selfish expectations they meet. So a major challenge is how preaching houses run by threatened ministers can be turned into trustful communities.

With the demise of the individualistic Enlightenment mind-set, the seeds of which also formed the context in which the Reformation took place, Free Church Christians have to face up to certain issues for the first time. For example:

- Our connectedness with the web of life in church and creation as a whole.
- Our continuity with the church that preceded our foundation.
- Our identity, if it is no longer defined by those we are against.
- Our cultural conditioning. The Bible tells of incarnation in a particular culture. How are we meant to be incarnate in today's culture?

The Church of Scotland

The Presbyterian Church is the most left-brained organisation in the world.

This was the conclusion of a Presbyterian minister who, realising in mid-life that he and his church were at a crossroads, had pilgrimaged to Ireland's ancient Celtic sites in search of inspiration. The agenda for people like him is how the Presbyterian Church can become as much right- as left-brained, a church in which intuition and human warmth, creative arts and contemplative prayer are offered to a post-modern generation that is more likely to find God, and to be sustained, through these avenues.

That prescient, if maverick, Church of Scotland divine, George McLeod, argued as long ago as the 1930s that with the collapse of the Puritan ideal, Presbyterianism needed to work out a new framework. His biographer observes he was arguing, 'that in order to go forward the Church must first go backwards, to ransack the drawers of its own past and find garments which would fit for today and tomorrow. From the Celtic Church he drew a sense of the totality of all life infused by the Spirit, from the Roman Catholic Church a sense of universality, from the Reformers the doctrine of the priesthood of all believers.' McLeod's vivid experience of Orthodox worship on Easter Day in Jerusalem was also a key. 'The combination of action, mystery and theatre had completely overwhelmed this inheritor of the Govan Scoto-Catholic tradition.' McLeod felt that post-Calvin Calvinism had taken the mystery out of the Faith. The kirk had forgotten that its Reformation mentor, John Knox, stood for daily church services, frequent communion and liturgical prayers; starved of symbols in their churches, Scots had turned to Freemasonry for ritual.[5]

The restoration of Iona's monastic living quarters by unemployed Glaswegians working with young ministers in training, and the formation of the Iona Community, created a vehicle which God has used to bring something of this transformation into being. At the turn of the millennium, it was obvious that the Church of Scotland as a whole had managed to accommodate the Iona Community with some pride, yet, apart from the use of its songs, had not allowed it to change its old frame of reference.

In the view of McLeod's biographer, Ronald Ferguson, the 1950s was the last era in which the kirk engaged with the central realities of Scottish political, social and cultural life on anything like an equal footing.

5. Ferguson, Ronald *George McLeod: Founder of the Iona Community* (William Collins, 1990).

Could it be that certain items on McLeod's agenda need now to be taken fully on board? The use of theatre in every locality; the restoration of daily worship; groups living among the poorest; developing a partnership of trust with other branches of the universal church. Although McLeod passionately defended the strengths of Calvin and Scottish Presbyterianism, he came to realise that 'its range of illumination was limited'.[6] The need now is to learn to honour spiritual leaders of other churches without being dominated by them.

Myth busters are needed in the Church of Scotland, for the Reformation has become an end road rather than a launching pad. 'The Reformation did away with one pope and replaced it with many,' was one minister's wry comment on the presbyteries of today. Presbyteries are too big. In their origin they were supportive cells, not legal courts, and they need to become so again. Congregations are strong institutions, and when the childlike faith of the founding Christians has been lost, they are often controlled by human wills which are unwilling to let God take over.

The fear of charismatic gifts needs to be overcome. A few congregations, inspired by charismatic renewal, have been able to restore 'Body ministry'. Newhills Church, in Aberdeen Presbytery, has practised 'Body Ministry' for many years, and members use the gifts of the Spirit in their everyday service of God. The healing ministry has resurfaced in not a few churches. A workmanlike understanding of spiritual gifts needs now to unfold more widely.

The ghost of monasticism has to be exorcised. The Church has assumed that monasticism depends upon

6. Ferguson, Ronald *George McLeod: Founder of the Iona Community*, (William Collins, 1990), p. 264.

celibacy, that celibacy is unbiblical, and therefore not in the Reformed tradition, and in any case Church of Scotland ministers have their rights to family houses. This approach eschews an option. Voluntary celibacy is, of course, biblical, and needs to be treated as an honoured option once again; but the communities that are needed will consist of married as well as of single people.

'The trouble is,' a leading Church of Scotland minister confides, 'the church is in denial.' The pew is out of touch with the clergy. Many clergy feel, 'Whatever it is we're supposed to be doing we're not doing it,' and spend their life bowed down by false guilt.

'I don't believe that you have to become twee, nice, docile, Benedictine or English to be a Christian,' a Scot told me. He continued: 'I believe Jesus must have been rugged and well built and a working man. He was in touch with his gut and could express it. So we Scots show we are Christians by "Rising up in the power of God" prayers; by being wild and manly and being in touch with the warrior in us; by being courageous and able to stand alone and reach out.' The challenge is to set free again the manly and womanly spirit underneath the church paraphenalia.

The church is fear bound. It fears losing control, it fears charismatic movements, and it fears post-modern cultures that flow past it. It needs the courage to look at the whole picture, to diagnose the actual spiritual condition of Scotland, the strengths and weaknesses of the church, and points where deep repentance and change are needed. In 1999 The General Assembly of the Church of Scotland asked Peter Neilson to head up a commission to advise on the shape of the church from 2001. Peter had been invited by St Cuthberts Church, Edinburgh, to become its minister to the unchurched. As he trod the streets by night as well as by day he learned this truth: 'Go to the place of your greatest fear and it will become the place of your greatest strength.' St Cuthbert's has begun to plant faith communities in non-church spheres such as clubland, and the Church of Scotland now has a website named 'churchwithoutwalls'.

Scotland could demonstrate what a God-controlled nation can do in the world.

The challenge to leaders of all churches

Many local church leaders are dispirited. They are dispirited by the mind-set of their congregations. 'Post-modern church-goers,' one minister told me, 'think they'll come to church when it suits them, but they expect it to be there for them. The minister is reduced to a supermarket checkout. The consumer mentality is killing both discipleship and the pastors. This mentality is an evil but few churchgoers recognise it as such. In the church it cannot be true that the customer is king: Jesus is King and we are to be the body that serves him.'

Ministers in mainstream churches are dispirited by the system and its leaders. Take one example – a curate pioneers a new work in a school or housing estate. Although the mother church is without its vicar, the bishop pulls out the curate because his standard three years is up. That fledgling and needy flock is left without a shepherd. That crassness is typical of shibboleths and straitjackets, which grind fine local church leaders into the ground. Many suffer burnout, resign or lose heart.

Some leaders confuse loving people with meeting their expectations. When this confusion is aligned to a low self-image it leads to disaster. Because they are not secure in their own identity in God, these leaders become hostage to what is not of God in their people.

Others confuse their own ego with God's will. A new minister came to his church with an exciting agenda which he believed was from God. Various members opposed this or that item. His instinctive reaction was to regard them as enemies, and his flow of love towards them dried up. The members intuited that their minister did not love them for themselves, but only if they were fodder for his plans. The minister realised this. He decided that, instead of laying 'his stuff' on to his congregation, he would love them for themselves, and help to draw out what was of God in 'their stuff'. It was not long before members realised this was 'a new deal' and started to love him.

Leaders can find God-given authority

The American psychologist Daniel Goleman, in his groundbreaking book, *Emotional Intelligence,* concludes that emotional rather than rational intelligence marks out the true leader. He claims that 'the very architecture of the brain gives feelings priority over thought'. Emerging church leaders know this.

The true servant leader is strong, not weak. A wise woman told me: 'What has departed from our culture is leaders who are strong, real. I am looking for leadership which is earthy, masculine, motherly and has a deep love which is reliable. An awful lot of godliness is up in the air. If you lean on it, it falls flat. Power corrupts. Absolute power corrupts absolutely.'

The Celtic church leaders had the physical courage to go out in front and vanquish monsters and evils. They did not play safe. They did not hide behind paper. Their humanity did not get squeezed out by the weight of top-heavy committees. Their vulnerability did not get covered over because they operated in the safety zones of boards or old-boy networks.

> Never trust a leader who walks without a limp.
> *John Wimber*

After St Cuthbert recovered from the plague he walked with a limp for the rest of his life. He was a strong leader, but I suspect this limp endeared him to the people.

The ability not to hide weakness is a mark of Christ-like leadership.

Some clergy are too comfortable or fearful to break out of the churchy framework which prevents them from sharing their people's vulnerability. When large numbers joined the church in the first millennium it became a large organisation. It then required money from members to pay for clergy who did the most significant jobs. This marginalised the lay people. Soon the clergy became acclimatised to comfort and to the corridors and assumptions of power. They had no idea what it felt like to be homeless and powerless. Vulnerability is a voluntary relinquishment of the power to automatically protect oneself from being wounded.

Mark Green, Vice-Principal of London Bible College, conducted research on public perceptions of preachers. What did he find people were looking for? 'Basically for spiritual wisdom to deal with the pressures and relationships of day-to-day life. What emerged most forcefully was the perception that the preacher was out of touch with people's lives. The advice section of the questionnaire was full of comments like: "Visit factories, nursing homes, schools. Go talk to the Labour Exchange. Read *The Sun*."' [7]

Diagnosis of the retreating church's leadership is easy. But what to do about it? How can a large Body of Christ serve the masses and yet remain personal and sensitive to

7. *Idea* Nov/Dec 1998. A fuller account of this research was published in *Anvil*, Vol. 14, No. 4, 1997.

changing needs? In the Celtic model, leadership was often given to those who renounced personal property and who were accountable to one another. Thus bishops were under the authority of a male or female leader of a monastery. In the emerging church, people are led by those who have a Rule of Life which involves renunciation of power.

The early Celtic churches at their best managed to do two apparently opposite things. On the one hand they released Christians who would wander off for the love of God, or work out their individual calling with the help of a soul friend. A bishop was given discretion to evangelise in any way that he felt was appropriate. He was a flying bishop, released from the burdens of church management to move in mission wherever the Spirit led. On the other hand, the Celtic churches fostered communities and a sense of belonging. The abbot was a true father of a large family, a focus of unity, a sign of life-long stability to the many people who lived nearby.

In the emerging church the pastor sees her/his role as releasing people into being fully human. Celtic-style bishops or translocal church leaders come alongside congregations and bless what God is blessing. Anglican bishops still retain a faint residue of this way of operating; they spend a year in mid-term visiting the people in and out of their churches, delegating, postponing or overlooking other duties.

Leaders in the emerging church are not afraid to use their intuition. They understand the soul of any venture. The soul of a venture is revealed in a crisis when façades are stripped away. Leaders define it; followers identify with it; the leader helps them to bond with it. [8] Leaders in the

8. This is explored in Joyner, Rick, *Leadership, Management and the Five Essentials for Success* (Morning Star Publications, 1600 Lancaster Highway, Charlotte, NC 28277 2062, USA 1995).

retreating church postponed the painful decisions which were necessary to turn things round, for fear of the short-term pain and controversy. Emerging church leaders grasp the nettle first of all, and then enjoy the fruits of peace and blessing. Leaders in the retreating church majored on minors; leaders in the emerging church majored on major.

In the imperial model of the church, a hierarchy can impose leaders who are unknown, lack rapport with their people and can therefore achieve little. The leaders of the Celtic Christian communities were the natural leaders of that people. This created problems when their heirs were less godly than those they led, but the system that replaced it, of clergy being outsiders appointed by authorities that seemed alien, was not the answer. Bishops in the early church, such as Martin of Tours and Cuthbert of Lindisfarne, were elected by the people. Popular technology now makes it possible for every church member in, say, a diocese, to vote for a candidate who they think should be considered. In today's Celtic Orthodox Church a candidate for Bishop is proposed and elected; he comes from the community. The introduction of local ordained ministers by other churches is a step in the right direction, but the system for assessing who should be ordained is class-ridden and myopic. In industry people are appointed according to their proven skills; the church still appoints people who pass paper exams but who lack leadership skills and rapport with people, and bypass many fine potential leaders who are neither called nor prepared to collude with a training system that is a travesty of true leadership.

I was not born into a family of leaders, nor was I bred in a public school that prides itself on leadership training. I missed compulsory conscription into the Armed Forces by three months, and the squashed child inside me did not know how to make effective relationships across the board in an adult world. My Church of England theological college provided me with no training in management, in interfacing with the statutory agencies or in how to handle inner primal material. Yet God had called me to be the founding minister in a significant housing development. I knew I could not abdicate my responsibility.

I recalled the words of an Iranian MP who was a guest when I was a curate in London: 'You are responsible for the spiritual welfare of all the people in this place.' Was I? I also recalled the words of a former English rugby player: 'You can grow in manhood by emulating Abraham, who talked through with God every decision he needed to take, and took it.' I made it my job to get training in missing skills at my own expense.

CHAPTER 7

Experiments

'The vision is great, but where is it happening?' asked a young Christian strategist. 'Maybe none of these new-style faith communities have been fully born yet,' I replied, 'but I have no doubt there are many embryos waiting to be born.' Monastic churches such as Taizé, in France; transformed parishes such as Medugorge, in Croatia, and avant-garde projects such as those Mike Riddell features in his book *Threshold of the Future* could be cited as examples. In this chapter I mention just five, the first four briefly and the fifth, a more extended account of the church I served as its first minister. I choose these examples, not because they have achieved everything, but because they are pregnant with possibilities.

Antioch Church, Llanelli, Wales

The skyline of the bustling South Wales town of Llanelli boasts plenty of church spires. Coming down to earth in its shopping centre you would not immediately notice an ordinary complex of buildings. Here there is a charity shop, which the low-paid frequent with pushchairs, and a hairdressing salon. Young people can skateboard outside, and enjoy a cyber café inside. Former drug addicts who have recently discovered their creativity, display their paintings and other artefacts in another room. One room is locked: a recording studio where local groups can rehearse and record. A larger auditorium can be used for most things, from aerobics to Sunday worship. There are kids' rooms and offices and a play area and so on. This is Antioch Church, a seven-day-a-week faith community that is a spiritual and social hub for the town. All sorts of people find a home there, even would-be monks. A Salvation Army Christian told them he wished to experiment with being a hermit, so he has a caravan not too far away, but values the church as his supportive umbrella. Does it address ecological issues? A former pagan earth warrior who lived entirely on natural sources in Tepee Valley is now a member of this church. He told me: 'When I became a Christian the Holy Spirit made me even closer to the earth than I was before.'

Church of the Saviour, Washington DC

The Church of the Saviour in Washington DC was founded by Gordon Crosby after World War II. Gordon learned the practice of silence at a Pennsylvania retreat centre, which was influenced by George McCleod, founder of the Iona Community. Gordon's vision was to create an Iona-type of base in the USA, mobilising theological students to build it. The disciplines taught included accountability to others for daily prayer and Scripture reflection.[1]

---

1. See *Call to Commitment* by Elizabeth O'Connor (an account of the Church of the Saviour) (Harper & Row, 1963).

Gordon Crosby started out as a Baptist, but sought close relationship with all Christian denominations. Each would-be member of the Church of the Saviour undergoes six courses in the School of Christian Living, and then prepares a statement of what Christ means to them, the practical disciplines they will keep (e.g. tithing), the un-Christlike areas of their life they require help with, and what they feel called to do. They then make a covenant with the members of the church, which all renew annually. Thus they have embraced a common Christian lifestyle, which they call 'integrity in membership'.

Each new member joins one of several groups on the basis of their aptitude. Each group is responsible for an area of life such as teaching, retreats, the library or ecology. Each member prays daily for the church to be guided into its next steps, and undertakes not to leave the church for any reason other than a call from God; in that event the whole church sends them out with their blessing.

This community of Christians is the hub: the homes are places of nurture. From the hub radiate various works of Christ in the arts and with the unemployed and the unchurched.

The Dayspring is their Retreat Centre in the country-side. Here the land is cultivated, Christian festivals are creatively celebrated and spiritually hungry people are nurtured. There is an Arts Centre, which certain members are responsible for. Other members commit to the coffee shop, which provides Christian hospitality in the market place. Others run work projects in depressed areas. Some choose to join the Rockside House congregation. This may mean they live in and serve an unchurched suburb. Other members staff the Remedial Centre where people with health and emotional problems come. Finally, there is

Sarah's Circle. The church bought a row of tenements for old people to live in. In the basement are stimulating activities that bring life to old people whom others had written off, reminiscent of the new life God gave Abraham's wife Sarah long after she was thought to be of childbearing age.

Communities of renewal – household churches

In the New Testament churches are sometimes called households. There were household monastic churches in succeeding centuries, such as that led by Macrina, sister of Bishop Basil of Caesarea. Household churches are surfacing again.

Andrew and Jane Fitz-Gibbon explored with Celtic-minded friends in the UK, and then with Anabaptist friends in USA, what a new monasticism might be in a contemporary culture. In the late 1990s they established their own home-based community church at Ithaca, New York State. This has about 25 members, including children, and two small linked communities. About 15 attend weekly Theology School.

Although they came from a charismatic and free-spirited background, their study of monasticism led them to two conclusions. First, small communities need spiritual parents. Second, small communities have to be deeply connected to the whole church. These two convictions led the Fitz-Gibbons to become abbot and abbess (a husband and wife leadership team) and to be ordained by a bishop within the apostolic succession. In 2001 their community and ministries were chartered as a jurisdiction under the archbishop of the Communion of Evangelical Episcopal Churches.

The Breakwater Community, Geelong, Australia is a 30-year-old suburban monastery with a rich ecumenical spirituality based on the contemplative monastic approach and the need to address personal and corporate evil. It includes married and single people, its worship has strong Orthodox elements and its buildings are owned by the Baptists.

Bowthorpe – a divine accident?

In the 1970s Bowthorpe, a collection of fields around some farm and church ruins on the western outskirts of Norwich, became three linked urban 'villages' which met together at those ruins, which now encompass shopping, health, church, youth, craft and police centres. These form the hub of the well-designed mix of council and private housing which make up the three villages.

In the village hall in January 1978 Anglican, Free and Roman Catholic Church leaders commissioned me, with the Christian Brethren, House Church, Pentecostals, Quakers and Salvation Army extending the right hand of fellowship, to establish one family of Christians who would carry out Christ's will for the neighbourhood. 'I suppose there has never been a service in this country which has been so well represented in the licensing of a minister as this one,' enthused the Bishop.

We, the first Christians of Bowthorpe, took this mandate as God-given. Some of those who had given the mandate, who had not thought through the implications, assumed that the old parallel-track denominationalism would take precedence over the organic growth of 'one family of Christians'. Indeed, such a freedom to be organic would not have been permitted there before or afterwards. 'Bowthorpe is a divine accident,' David Edwards, the Church of England's most perceptive historian, is reported to have said.

So 'the Christian Church in Bowthorpe' became a laboratory. These are some of the discoveries we made.

The first was about weaving together Christianity's separated strands. The church decided that the Lord's people should gather round the Lord's table on the Lord's day as an expression of our being one community (the Catholic strand); that Bible study, personal conversion and witness to Christ were necessary for all who became members (the Protestant strand); and that as a church we would invite and use the gifts and graces of the Holy Spirit (the Pentecostal strand).

Protestants were becoming sacramental. Peter Groom, one of our preachers, put it like this: 'Some believe that Christ is on the table, all of us believe that He is at the table.' Isn't that sufficient basis for all to receive the Lord in this way? Moreover, when Protestants discovered that God could heal physical bodies at Holy Communion, it became no big deal to believe God's Spirit could transform matter, including bread and wine.

Since we had espoused the Pentecostal gifts, we invited Pentecostals to look upon us as the Pentecostal church for the area. The Orthodox were not formally linked to the church, since they barely had a presence in the city when we began. However, the presence of icons in our prayer room and the Orthodox custom of kissing the Cross became a regular option at our Friday night Prayer round the Cross.

There were also weavings to do with the procedures of our sponsoring denominations and there were sacramental weavings. The leaders of Norfolk churches had opposing views on baptism, and could not give us united guidance, so we agreed a policy with our Sponsoring Body based upon the report of the world's Churches, *Baptism, Eucharist and Ministry*. This recognised the baptism of each person who had accepted Jesus as Lord and who had either been baptised and later confirmed, or baptised as a believer. On the one hand there would be no indiscriminate infant baptism, and on the other hand those who had been baptised as infants would not have to be rebaptised. Christians were encouraged to renew their baptism, and this could include sprinkling or immersion in water.

Baptisms by immersion of new, unbaptised Christians were thrilling occasions, which drew in fresh people, uplifted the congregation, and accorded with the teaching, if not the practice, of all sponsoring denominations. We produced a people-friendly Service of Blessing and Dedication of Infants which gave parents virtually everything they wanted, including godparents, christening gowns, a naming ceremony, a celebration and a certificate.

A Churches Evaluation Report on Bowthorpe stated in 1993: 'The initiation practices at Bowthorpe have, in our judgement an integrity, as an interim solution . . . which deserve understanding and acceptance. We recommend . . . the (national) Churches to provide services that enable candidates to re-appropriate their baptism and that this process includes evidence from Bowthorpe . . .'

God gave me a love for the distinctive, God-given charism of each of the church streams, and I felt I was to make these part of my own life. These charisms had become bolted on to the rigid and rusting scaffolding of the denomination concerned, but now God was calling us to prise the charism free so that it could run its course freely. The charism was to be like yeast in the dough of the whole Christian church. Methodism's special gifts to the whole church seemed to be John Wesley's scriptural holiness, passion for mission, and the opportunity to make decisions democratically. Liberty of conscience and the church meeting was a Baptist charism. The ability to gather around the Word of God freed from institutional baggage and to respond flexibly was a URC charism. The charism of the Roman Catholic Church is obedience: obedience to Jesus in the ministers and sacraments of His Body, who safeguard its unity and focus community. Cherishing that which is of God in each person, and listening to that which is of God in oneself, were Quaker charisms. Being the church that provides hospitality for all these traditions and for all the people of this land was a Church of England charism. These charisms, of course, were hidden by much other baggage, but I felt they were the charisms to be embraced and lived until they were organic.

Sometimes our interweavings could be fun. One day Vera, a member of the Religious Society of Friends, one of our six sponsoring denominations, informed me in no uncertain terms that she was *not* prepared to be called a miserable sinner (a term used in the Church of England's *Book of Common Prayer*). My reply so amused her that she spread it around Norfolk's Quaker Meetings: 'You may not be miserable but you are a sinner all right!'

Any person called to found God's work in a new area must lay down their life for its people. 'A shepherd lays his life down for the sheep,' said Jesus (John 10:11). I recognised that my love must be unconditional; I had to be a sign of faithfulness to a rootless population.

Jesus said, 'You cannot serve two masters,' but many of my ordained colleagues were being pulled in contrary directions. This was the result of imaging their ministry as a career, or of their spouse pursuing a career unrelated to their own calling, or of sending their children, for the sake of their future careers, to schools unconnected with their area. Although I had the advantage of being celibate, I knew only too well how many things, even within a person, can pull them in contrary directions. I had to let go of everything, including my dreams, until nothing but the gift of God's call remained at the core of my being.

Among our sponsoring denominations Baptists and United Reformed churches cherished this concept of the shepherds being in covenant with their flocks. The Church of England, which used to, was bent on marginalising 'the parson's freehold' so it could move clergy around like pawns on a managerial chessboard, but fortunately I did have the freehold. The Methodists waived their policy of circulating ministers, and I was free to be a spiritual parent to the people of Bowthorpe.

After three years we formalised some foundations: decisions would be made in submission to the written Word of God, interpreted by the Holy Spirit, in the belief that Jesus Christ would speak to us and guide us if we seek Him; we would have an open-door policy to all the residents, welcome as members all who made a commitment to Christ, meet in groups, build one another up in love, develop every-member ministry, relate to each of the three villages and encourage the use of spiritual gifts.

The model of church that burned in founding members was that of the early Jerusalem Christians who met daily for prayer, shared food in their homes with generous hearts, praising God and having favour with all the people (Acts 2:44-47). I had read somewhere that 'community is a place where the connections felt in the heart make themselves known in bonds between people.' I felt certain that what the Church needed, more than new institutions or programmes, was to create Christian community – not to become a 'Community Church' on the basis of attraction to like-minded Christians who neglected to relate to fellow Christians in their neighbourhood. That kind of church often failed to renew the neighbourhood where it worshipped. Our church was meant to be to the neighbourhood what the heart is to the body.

Nevertheless it is a humanly impossible leap from our individualistic churches and society to the Christian community life that is needed to turn a neighbourhood God-wards. I had to accept that this is possible only if a range of factors is in place, and only if a deep work of God takes place.[2]

At first we each brought our different masks and jargon, which made our gatherings uncomfortable; but as we accepted one another, warts and all, we grew in unity-in-diversity, which is true community.

Our aim was that church programmes were inspired by members, members were not steamrollered into a church blueprint.

We sought a core of church members called to be available through the week within a common framework of prayer and service. A number of people bought a house in Bowthorpe in obedience to God, even against their own inclination, in order to become available in this way. Some lived very simply rather than take a full-time salary; others took retirement. A few committed themselves to daily public prayer together. Others took responsibility for pastoral care of the neighbourhood and the church.

We developed a commonly accepted lifestyle. This included ways of dealing with disagreements: do not criticise an individual in front of others; forgive others, even if you

2. An audit which enables one to determine whether these factors are in place is detailed in Appendice 4 of the Study Guide to this book.

disagree with them; deal with a fault in someone by talking it through face to face, always seeking the spiritual progress of the other person.

We also emulated this item in the Rule of the Taizé Community: 'Express in a few words what you feel conforms most closely to God's plan, without imagining that you can impose it.'

We waited on God for a vision. We knew that we were to build one family of Christians for one neighbourhood, and that this family was called to create an environment of love where the hurting people would find healing. We included all the members in the process of deepening, enlarging and updating the vision. Eventually the entire church drew up a vision statement entitled 'Christ for the Community: The Community for Christ'.

As we searched for the right headline phrase we thought of our early call to love the people of the neighbourhood and our later call to locate our physical presence where the three villages met. The phrase 'A Heart for Bowthorpe' emerged. We produced a logo depicting the three villages with a heart in their middle. Inside the heart two hands (one black, one white) were clasped in friendship around a Cross. This logo was reproduced on a banner that hangs in the Worship Centre and graces the cover of the monthly neighbourhood magazine, which goes to every home.

In early days we opened a shop unit each day in the first village of Clover Hill and named it 'The Open Door'. The secret of its success was that someone lived over the shop. The church was seen to be a home in the midst of the people. We realised this when a screaming young woman sought sanctuary one night before Christmas. As we locked the door behind her she told us her boyfriend was chasing her with a knife and would kill her. But before their quarrel began he had also told her, 'If ever you're in real trouble you can always go to The Open Door.'

We used the village hall for our Sunday morning worship, and at first rejected the idea of a building just for church activities, but we came to realise that both a congregation and the whole neighbourhood need a spiritual home. We were led to establish a Worship and Work area around the church and farm ruins at the centre of the three villages. Robin Manley Williams opted for a three-day week in the Civil Service in order to voluntarily oversee the building of a new Worship Centre. Certain church members established Bowthorpe Community Trust, which renovated the two farm cottages next to the Worship Centre for the use of members committed to this vision. Barbara Fox, a Franciscan tertiary, lived in one and the Tomlinson family in the other. The Trust purchased and renovated old harness rooms nearby and made them into wood workshops for people with learning difficulties and a craft shop where local folk could sell their crafts and find a listening ear. Peter Tomlinson became the manager.

Denominational leaders became patrons and Michael Handley, Archdeacon of Norwich, concluding that 'this project is so hare-brained it might just be of the Holy Spirit' became Chair of Trustees.

Barbara Fox was a new resident who, after joining the church, rediscovered a childhood longing to become a nun. She became a Franciscan tertiary, sold her new house and became warden of the small retreat cottage next to the Worship Centre. As a contemplative deeply committed to the place, she became a sign of God's faithfulness to a root-less generation. Others 'just moved' to Bowthorpe but, once there, also became signs by making themselves fully present to the neighbourhood for the sake of Christ.

We persuaded the Diocese to build Church House, where I lived, opposite the cottages. My sister Sally used the top floor; Raffaele Zuppardi, a former Verona Brother and separated from his wife, with his two children staying at weekends, completed the household community. For a time seven people met fortnightly to explore whether they were called to adopt a common Rule of Life. Since some of these were Roman Catholics, I sought the advice of Alan Clark, Roman Catholic Bishop of East Anglia. He was in favour of a Rule of Life shared by Christians of different church traditions, so long as it required each to be loyal to their own church. As it turned out, God moved most of the seven on.

In order to make the Worship Centre a spiritual home to the neighbourhood we made sure the design was welcoming, the chairs were comfortable and that there were refreshment, crèche, nappy changing, disabled, office and children's facilities. It became quite well used and was open every though not all day. Activities revolved around daily, Taizé-style morning and evening prayer. We sometimes had shared lunches or days together.

I was encouraged when a member told us on his return from Medugorge: 'It was like walking into a warm womb, and I feel like that about our church, too.'

We tried, in unobtrusive ways, to build listening into the fabric of our life together. We had times of silent listening in our meetings and worship. On fifth Sundays we shared in Quaker meetings, when nothing was spoken unless it was thought to be a prompting of God. Periodically we held a vigil when anyone could write, on an acetate, anything they felt God was saying to the church. Occasionally a member offered a prophetic word, which the leadership weighed and conveyed to the church.

A lunchtime prayer group listened to God on behalf of the church and neighbourhood. Sometimes they would sense pain in a particular part of Bowthorpe, and would pray at that place. They 'picked up' the pain of one street where crime and violence was taking over, and prayer-walked it. Days later a street resident was arrested; it was revealed he had been the local drugs ringleader with a mafia-like influence. Life improved for that street.

The idea of the whole church discovering God's marching orders by listening to the neighbourhood's pains and aspirations was new to evangelical members, who wondered how God could speak to people who did not worship him. We were a long way from the whole church owning this approach, but we took a hesitant step or two towards becoming a church that listens to the people. These commitments were included in the Vision Statement that the church eventually adopted: 'We cherish that which is of God in each person. We value everyone because God wants to be Father to them. We listen attentively.'

If we believed that the church in a neighbourhood is like a heart in a body, how could the church (the heart) bring renewal to the body (the neighbourhood)? We realised it could not do this if it was detached from the arteries of the body, which were the formal and informal neighbourhood networks. Yet how could we avoid the opposite danger of getting on to a treadmill of neighbourhood activities, which would eventually leave both us and the neighbourhood exhausted? A visiting preacher gave us a key: Osmosis. Osmosis is a biological process that echoes the process of human friendship. As local Christians draw in human life from the friends they make in the natural course of events (neighbours, shopping, schools, groups, pubs, sports, etc.) so their friends in turn imbibe their life, which is permeated by Christ. Christ in the believer filters out impurities that would otherwise be imbibed.

A residents' magazine was started, and soon church people were asked to run it, which they have done ever since.

Healing centre

Soon after I arrived I invited the Clover Hill doctors to lunch. Our resources were meagre compared to theirs, but we told them of a church member who could offer some counselling and of a group who met weekly to intercede for the sick. The doctors offered a room in their surgery, free of charge, for the counselling; and they asked us to keep a record of answers to our prayers for the sick, and to let them know the results. This we did, and it built up our faith. They also suggested we keep a Book of Remembrance in which could be recorded the names of loved ones who had died. On the anniversary of a bereavement, people often went to the doctor, feeling depressed. At their suggestion, we visited the bereaved at this time.

We accepted John Wimber's challenge in the 1980s that churches should routinely expect God to heal. We drew up guidelines and commissioned a healing ministry team and offered laying on of hands after every service.

A large health centre was built across the car park, by the Worship Centre. We developed teamwork with this, and health visitors recommended people to our parenting skills courses.

We wanted the church to be relevant to social needs, and to be seen as a resource by poor and professional residents alike, and by agencies such as schools and Social Services. We appointed a Voluntary Church Assistant at our Voluntary Aided Church Middle School, and were involved in other local schools. Church members started or sustained playgroups, monthly services in each of the five Sheltered Housing Centres and in a Nursing Home. Some of our members turned a village hall into a classy Saturday Night Dive for young people, which they named Twisters. The same people purchased a large derelict barn from the City Council with the aim of turning it into a Leisure and Community Centre. The barn had to be razed, but in its place are plans for a community peace garden.

Cherish animals and earth

Once two of us were praying for someone who was hurting. He and I sat each side of a sofa with Lucy the dog between us. He went limp as we invited the Holy Spirit to rest upon him. We had not anticipated, however, that our prayer would have the same effect on Lucy. She went so limp that she fell on to the floor and lay there, out to the world. God was teaching us that ordinary churches are to bless animals.

And the earth. A new resident knocked on my door. 'I stopped going to churches because they do not honour the earth,' Judith explained. 'I tried New Age and American Indian communities who do honour the earth, but I left them because they do not honour Christ. I am looking for a church that honours both Christ and the earth.' 'Come and help us,' I told Judith, who began to care for the plants around the church ruin.

Although we had no churchyard, we created a garden of remembrance where ashes are scattered. Shortly afterwards we held our first annual Blessing of the Earth service. Afterwards, a new member, Gary, who had gained sensitivity through suffering, said: 'Something has changed. Now the earth of Bowthorpe can breathe freely again after all these years.'

At the second such service, in a dell, we were joined by some gypsy children. They helped to fasten a banner in the ground, proclaiming 'Bowthorpe, the Community for Christ'. It was a symbolic offering back of the land to God, in partnership with those whose families had lived there long before the houses were built.

Roots matter

David Parker, the Vineyard Churches' prophetic leader from North America, was giving a talk at a Day of Renewal in Bowthorpe. He used a phrase of London Underground announcers, 'Mind the gap', as his theme for talks around the country. He would urge his hearers to mind the gap between the church and the people, between the Bible and their behaviour, and so on. As he spoke at Bowthorpe he suddenly looked at a glass seat we had placed in an alcove of this modern Worship Centre, beneath which the foundations of an ancient Saxon church could be seen. 'I have never said this before in my talks,' David said, 'but I feel very strongly the Lord has drawn to my attention the following point: mind the gap between your ancient roots and the present.'

We decided to research and produce an illustrated booklet on Bowthorpe's ancient and modern history to help people 'mind the gap'. [3]

Housing estates need saints

Few Bowthorpe church members were 'into' saints. However, during a sabbatical pilgrimage to the wooden cell of

3. Simpson, Ray *Bowthorpe, a Community's Beginnings*
   (Open Door Publications, 1982). Available at £1.50 plus p & p
   from The Hobby Horse, Bowthorpe Hall Road, Bowthorpe,
   Norwich NR1 9AA.

Switzerland's national saint, the farmer Nicholas of Flue, one of those rare and unmistakable commands from God came to me. I must turn a ruined blacksmith's forge on the site scheduled to become a vicarage into a rustic prayer cell. It must be dedicated to a nearby Norfolk saint, who was also a layman and a farm worker, as well as a healer, namely St Walstan.

Jeremy Dearling offered to make a sculpture of St Walstan, which would also tell the inspiring story of Walstan to passers by; the sculpture was sponsored by local industries. This was a private venture of mine, and misunderstandings had to be talked through. The Bishop of Lynn, David Bentley, dedicated the cell to God during the Week of Prayer for Christian Unity, 'for the transformation of the collective unconscious life of the neighbourhood'.

Then Rabbi Lionel Blue, who was making a TV series on holy places of East Anglia, heard about the cell and insisted on bringing his weary film crew over. 'Jews aren't supposed to believe in saints,' he told us before he sat, lost in thought, before Walstan. Suddenly he spoke, as if making an announcement to the world: 'Walstan is the answer to the yuppie. Every housing estate needs a saint.' The film crew went home, but Lionel's words live on.

Eldred Willey, a church member and a journalist for *The Tablet*, wrote an article about God's healing presence coming into the broken lives of people in the workshops next to St Walstan. This was happening, he thought, because St Walstan had been invited back into the area. Another resident pictured the farm worker Walstan as being allowed by God to 'dig the soil of the hearts of the people of Bowthorpe', creating a God-consciousness in the neighbourhood. When two teenagers, who were widely known as lovable rogues, were killed riding a stolen motorbike, a whole generation of local young people were affected. It was to the Prayer Cell that many of them came, to grieve, to sit, to think, to pray, to place a flower or a note. Care was needed to prevent the cell being used as a hideout for crime. To maintain its accessibility to all and sundry was a calculated risk, but one worth the taking. Children, shoppers, trolley-men from the local supermarket, dog-walkers and others not directly connected with the church felt at ease enough to become still within its rough walls.

Angels and evil

I had prepared for my new ministry at Bowthorpe by listening to a cassette course for pastors by Jack Hayford, Pastor of the Pentecostal Church on the Way, Los Angeles. When his ministry there began the church was quite small and rather dingy. Believing that the Lord is 'enthroned on the praises of his people' (Psalm 22:3) Jack and his pastoral team met in their church on Saturday nights to pray for the Sunday services. On one such night he felt they were being told to station themselves at the four corners of the sanctuary, and to extend their hands as though lifting up a canopy of praise. A sense of God's presence enveloped them. On repeating this another Saturday the building filled with a smoke-like golden aura; it seemed to them like the 'Shekinah glory' that long before had filled Israel's temple. Next day, though nothing was outwardly different from previous weeks, the congregation doubled. As the pastors reflected on this, they concluded that there were four angelic beings stationed at the same locations as the four pastors. 'The angelic beings had not taken their stations at our address,' one of them commented, 'rather, our commitment to worship had aligned us with God's address.'[4]

4. Hayford, Jack *The Church on the Way* (Zondervan, 1985).

The fact that a Pentecostal Church had learned to align its worship with the eternal worship of heaven brought a flicker of hope that this might be possible in a place such as Bowthorpe. Some Saturdays one of our worship team or myself walked the Worship Centre with uplifted hands forming a canopy of praise; later our Associate Minister did the same.

When a faith-sharing team from St Andrew's Church, Chorleywood, visited us, their leader David Pytches commented that the building had been released and was free for praise. One of our older members, Joyce, told me she heard monks singing during our worship time. Afterwards I discovered that the site of our modern Worship Centre had once been a monastery chantry.

Churches, like cities and individuals, either go forward or they go backward. Teenage vandalism threatened to turn the 'dream village' of Bowthorpe into a nightmare. Yuppies, including church members, moved out. Many who stayed had too low an image of themselves and of Bowthorpe to halt a downward spiral. In such a situation, how should a church carry out Jesus' injunction to overcome evil with good? We sought a God-given strategy with good people who wanted to turn the situation round. Head teachers, police, youth workers, voluntary organisations, health and church workers met together. The approach was three-pronged: To raise residents' self-image, to make personal contact with the vandals and to get the whole church praying.

I have not reported the weaknesses of myself and the church. The reason is that there were so many! The lesson is that because we were so vulnerable God had a chance to do something!

History is littered with churches that began as a movement and ended as a monument. A regular visitor to

Bowthorpe told me that most churches he returned to after a period away had not changed; they seemed stuck in a time warp. He felt that we were a living organism; and he noticed that there were little adaptations, creative responses to fresh insights, people, circumstances or seasons.

The Church is Christ's Body. Christ walked with God every day of his life. So must the Church. In order for churches to be God's journeying people they must listen to their dreams.

I had a dream. It was so powerful that it came back day after day. The whole of Bowthorpe turned out for a funeral. It was the funeral of a person named 'Mr Bowthorpe'. The crowds went in procession down to the crematorium. And I, Ray Simpson, led the procession.

Eighteen years before, God had told me to lay down my life for Bowthorpe. Now he was telling me I had to die to Bowthorpe, or else it would become an idol. God was moving me on.

I knew that Bowthorpe was a halfway house towards the Church that is meant to emerge in Britain and that it needed ordained leaders with fresh energies and skills to take it forward.

CHAPTER 8

Cells, Congregations, Communities – Villages of God

We have explored the spirituality, challenges and some examples of the emerging church. What about its shape? The second-millennium church was based on order, and feared letting its members 'go with the flow'.

In the end it became a prisoner of its own framework. Chaos theory in science reveals, however, a creative interaction between fluid particles, which become life enhancing. The emerging church seeks flexible frameworks, which enable all people to move and grow and flow with God's Spirit within the natural patterns around them.

The signs of potential in the emerging church seem to lie in two poles, both of which are more flexible than the traditional church: the small house unit and the hub. Middle-sized congregations, which are just trying to 'keep something going', are in steep decline and need to adapt or die.

So let us look at the small, the middle-sized and the hub churches.

Cells and groups

A growth point in the world church is the upsurge in cell churches. Evidence from Canada suggests, however, that these do better in new situations than they do when grafted on to long-established congregations. Nevertheless, certain congregations in the main streams are developing cells as their way forward.

This is, for them, a rediscovery of the central role that the relationally based small group is meant to have within the Church. These are not the traditional home groups, but real Christian mini-communities who put God at the centre of who they are and what they do. Pioneers such as Ralph Neighbour, Bill Beckham and certain Korean church leaders offer various expressions of cell church.

Cells provide for more intimate sharing, study, prayer and friendship than can a Sunday congregation. They enable certain tasks to be accomplished in mission or community care, and they provide for the pastoral needs of each member. They can restore a sense of 'ownership' to the members of the church.

There are, however, limits to what cells can achieve. Sometimes a cell is presented as being comparable to a family, but an arbitrary allocation of Christian brothers and sisters cannot do justice to their deepest needs, bonds and inner journeys. The aim of cells is to add to their numbers and form new cells, but they thereby lose continuity. Many Christians are too stressed or wounded to cope with such artificial change. A family does not jettison members when it grows, and it has times for all the family to be together or to be remembered. Cells can alienate families if children are excluded, and older people if children are included.

Some people find the cell too small a unit to allow them

to cope with an over-demanding member. Some cell leaders never bargained for the demands that deplete their reservoir of energy or skill.

Cells fail to meet the need of the general public for a visible contact point for the local church. Local authorities, schools, media, other churches, funeral directors, wedding couples, social services, police, newly arrived local residents, travellers, people in crisis, seekers after spirituality do not know where to look if cells are the only expression of church. Free-ranging souls do not wish to be constrained by such units. If they have no other focus to relate to they will lose their church connection.

These qualifications apply also to traditional home groups, and to the increasing number of cross-church, ad hoc groups that are not grounded in any one church.

To handle this challenge successfully cell members need to relate to a wider framework, which gives them more space, choice, stability, cross-weaving, coherence and support.

Where can this sustained framework be found?

Middle-sized congregations

Not, as a rule, in the middle-sized congregation. In many urban and sparsely populated rural areas the middle-sized church structure has come to the end of its shelf life. A Church Survey of 1999 predicted that half of these churches would close. To operate as the church for the area, having to supply all the things a church is expected to provide, takes more money, time, organisation, talent, motivation and numbers than these congregations have, or can be expected to have. Buildings that are too expensive or cumbersome to sustain, bleed the life out of the dwindling few who try to maintain them.

Denominations still try to prop up these non-viable

institutions – the Church of England amalgamates existing parish structures, and puts non-stipendiary ministers into empty vicarages, not to generate new forms of life, but to perpetuate the old. The subsidised paid clergy who are asked to manage these expanded bureaucratic shells say they have an untenable job. Many suffer stress or resign, but they are often not listened to. This is manifestly not the way ahead.

Post-modern church members, who in other areas of life are free to follow multiple choices, are made to feel guilty because they do not wish to be tied to the organisation of such a church. These Christians increasingly realise that God does not mean them to waste their lives propping up what is wrong. They are voting with their feet and their pockets.

The eyes and noses and ears in the Body of Christ now know that if there is to be a People's Church, Christians must adopt, not only a new spirituality, but also organic structures that reflect and sustain this. They are no longer willing to collude with structures weighted to preserve what is untenable. They know that obsolete church structures that are more of a drain than a resource must be allowed to die. So non-viable middle-sized churches need to stop trying to be what they are not and to become what they are meant to be. They need to discern the nature of their context and their calling. What are the options?

Many middle-sized churches must close

Many small to middle-sized congregations have little future as they are, and need to close. Their remaining members need to find a specific but limited role in their locality. The few Christians who worship in such churches have a role to play as a Christian presence in that area, but to relate to a hub in the wider church. They need to discern what shape that Christian presence should take. A house fellowship? A monthly family service in a school or community centre? Alternative worship in a dance hall? A spirituality course? A children's club or school?

Some middle-sized churches should be recycled

One church might become a group of homes, which warm their village through their hospitality. Another might meet in a church building of ancient foundation, and keep daily corporate prayer going on a rota basis. Another might develop creative arts and workshops.

Under-used church buildings sited in natural gathering places can be recycled as multi-resource centres. St Paul's at The Crossing, Walsall, was looking redundancy in the face, yet was sited in the middle of the town centre. It sold the ground level of its site to eight shop owners; on the second level the church has a café, a drop in centre and a chapel; on the third level is the worship centre, which is used by many groups on weekdays. There is public daily prayer in the chapel, which is much used by shoppers for private prayer. Certain rural church buildings can become local retreat centres, and a small rota can maintain daily prayer. One Norfolk church advertised for a hermit.

Some middle-sized congregations are viable as they are

They have life and leadership, few 'artificial' overheads, and they fit their locality. New Life Church, in Alnwick, Northumberland has only about 50 members, but it has a committed all-age congregation, few overheads (it meets in a school), a viable catchment area (Alnwick is a market town) and a big vision. Their vision is to buy the old Corn Exchange and make it a hub for the life of the town, trusting other Christians and people of goodwill to play their part.

The Church of England is at its best in market towns, and in certain smaller areas parish churches are restoring the practice of daily worship and building annexes that offer everyday facilities.

Some middle-sized churches can become neighbourhood churches

St Barnabas, Inham Nook, Nottingham is close to the pub, shops, clinic and school in a housing estate with serious social problems. Unlike the early monastic churches, the church does not own these other facilities, but its members animate them. The pub is the social arm of the church, the fish and chip shop the supplier of food for its gatherings. Church members are the heart and soul of the pub, and bring new-made friends over to the church. On a visit there I met Simon, a young former drug addict who had horribly slashed his face and feet. He found the church people so friendly in the pub that he accepted Jesus into his life that day. Many folk on the estate were out of work, heavy smokers, or on medication. These habitually went both to the doctor and to the church. Medicine, care and prayer were not in separate compartments, they were part of a whole. Thus members received prayer for healing and found help, they attended the clinic, and on their return found someone who would care for them. Pete, who could not get paid employment, was a volunteer carer for a mother with lung cancer. He brought her to church and she asked me to pray for strength for that week. St Barnabas knew that it is no good just turning a church into a hive of activities. Every day began with simple, Celtic-style prayer.

St Patrick's Church, in downtown Hove, Sussex had a large Victorian building, which was nearly redundant. The Bishop of Chichester invited four monks from the

Community of the Servants of the Will of God to buy a nearby three-storey terraced house. They transferred three of their daily services of worship into the church. The monks gave homeless and hungry people hospitality, according to their Rule, but they had too little room to meet the need. So the rear of the church building was converted into a shelter for the homeless and meals were provided following the midday and evening services. Pews were removed and icons put in their place. Soon not only the poor attended daily prayer, but business people in suits came out of the woodwork too.

Father Gregory, abbot of the community of the Servants of the Will of God, believes that the mediaeval monasteries went wrong when they lost the link between the monastery and the neighbourhood and failed to pass on the principles of Christian community life to the church at large. In the light of the link between their monastic house and St Patrick's he wrote *Living for the Kingdom: a Rule for the Parish Community*, which integrates all aspects of church life into the daily pattern of dying and rising with Christ.

The church in the village of Stanton-by-Dale, Derbyshire, turned two redundant schools into a new independent church school and a church centre, a redundant air-raid shelter into a post office/shop run by a charitable trust and a disused Methodist chapel into a visitor and conference centre.

There cannot be one monochrome blueprint, for each situation is different. There will be and should be diversity, but one thing seems clear. If the former middle-sized congregations who have become Christian presences or recycled centres are to survive and flourish, they need to be part of something bigger. They need to be like a spoke in a wheel. They need to relate to a hub.

Hub churches

There is a groundswell of Christians who put their energies into groups or networks rather than into congregations. The UK Christian Directory expands yearly to accommodate the entries of ever more networks. While church attendance declines, Christian initiatives increase. But how can they avoid being like the over-individualistic people in Moses' day, when everyone 'did what was right in their own eyes'? Some Christians follow an individual path, which keeps them on the move, uninvolved in the day-to-day life of a church. Like spokes in a wheel, they long for a hub to which they can relate. So also do many small churches. They don't respond to being slotted into some bureaucratic arrangement; they need an organic relationship with a spiritual home. As more middle-sized churches close, the remaining groups of Christians will want to make links with hubs.

So large numbers of Christian groups, networks, small churches, as well as mobile Christians outside them, cannot flourish unless there are also centres of stability, prayer, resource and hospitality to which they may relate. But what form should these hubs take?

We need more than celebration networks

In the 1980s the concept developed of cell – congregation – celebration. The celebration was the occasional coming together of congregations, and was probably arranged by the headquarters of the umbrella network. This was not holistic. Congregations felt used. A hub church enables celebrations, but it is much more than that.

We need more than umbrella churches

In the same period certain large, lively churches planted and nurtured new churches, and offered resources to them.

Struggling, or merely small, congregations began to relate to them as umbrella churches. Churches such as Holy Trinity, Brompton, St. Andrew's, Chorleywood, or St Thomas Church, Crookes, Sheffield provide training days, faith-sharing teams, courses and consultancies. For these things they should be blessed. A hub church is, indeed, a resourcing umbrella church, but it is even more than that. If umbrella churches are to become holistic hubs they need to address how to provide an experience of lived community, unprogrammed space, daily corporate rhythm and guest accommodation. Faith communities of other religions are ahead of the game.

We need more than multi-resource centres

We have noted how some middle-sized congregations have turned their buildings into multi-resource centres. Some large churches have done the same. Kingsway Centre, near Liverpool, is open every day and provides a café, children's facilities, counselling, prayer and much else, staffed by members of the Kingsway church. Such places are a blessing. A hub church is a multi-resource centre, but it is more than that. For its members do not live private lives away from their church centre. A hub church is organic.

We need more than minster churches

Nick Spencer, a consultant for the Henley Centre, is one of several voices calling for a recovery of the minster system. As the church struggles with unsuitable church buildings and untenable parish boundaries, it needs to remember that for most of the first millenium the minster was the basic unit of pastoral care in England.

The typical minster, however, was a clerical set-up; it was not of, by and for the people.

Calls for 'people's monastery churches' – the new monasticism

Just as the inescapable need for holistic hub churches stares us in the face, a fresh generation is questing after a new monasticism. I believe that nothing less than a modern, people-friendly form of monastic church can do what is needed.

Unchurched people who seek spirituality with integrity will not buy into churches whose primary dynamic is to preserve or extend the institution. They will buy into a model of church that engenders trust, rhythm and hospitality – and this is the monastic pattern that is increasingly being called for.

The German evangelical church martyr, Dietrich Bonhoeffer, wrote in a prophetic letter to his brother Karl in January 1935:

> The restoration of the Church must surely come from a new kind of monasticism, which will have only one thing in common with the old, a life lived without compromise according to the Sermon on the Mount in the following of Jesus. I believe the time has come to gather people together for this.' [1]

While he was pastoring German-speaking Christians in London during Hitler's regime, the Confessing Church invited Bonhoeffer to establish an underground seminary for the Confessing Church at Finkenwalde. On receiving this invitation Bonhoeffer asked Bishop Bell to advise him of monasteries he could visit in England. One of these, Mirfield, impressed him with its emphasis on the regular

1. Quoted in Mary Bosanquet, *The Life and Death of Dietrich Bonhoeffer* (Hodder & Stoughton 1968), chapter XI.

daily offices of prayer, and the frequent repetition of the psalms. At Finkenwalde he trained four sets of ordinands in the context of a praying community.

Despite his aristocratic limitations Bonhoeffer introduced a significant new dynamic into the Protestant Church. Academic study had been divorced from devotion since it had been taken out of the monasteries and put into largely secular universities. At Finkenwalde the *lectio divina* was restored. Students allowed God to speak directly to them as they spent time each day in silent reflection on a Bible passage. Bonhoeffer also restored the practice of confession to a senior colleague, and thus also a sense of discipline and accountability.

During this period he wrote three books: *Discipleship, Life Together* and *Spiritual Care.* These yield clues to what he envisaged. He believed that you do not make community, you enter into what is already given.

Because of his execution in a prison cell shortly before the end of World War II we shall never know how he would have developed a new monasticism had he survived. Sadly, the German Church did not take hold of what he had conceived. In Scotland, however, George McLeod had been developing the Iona Community during those same war years. Bonhoeffer's *Life Together* became standard reading there.

A generation after Bonhoeffer the evangelical leader John Stott called for 'the re-monking' of the church. In this decade Eugene Petersen has called on Protestant church leaders to be radical, and to make a calculated plan to replace their 'ego lust to be god' with a corporate pattern that makes space for God. He writes:

Historically the most conspicuous corporate construction that does this is the monastery . . . The genius of the monastery is its comprehensiveness; all the hours of the day are defined by prayer; all the activity of the monks is understood as prayer . . . This external comprehensiveness penetrates community and soul.' He quotes Oxford historian Herbert Butterfield, who wrote, 'Sometimes I wonder at dead of night whether, during the next fifty years, Protestantism may not be at a disadvantage because a few centuries ago it decided to get rid of monks.' Petersen calls for 'an open monastery', and concludes: 'What is critical is an imagination large enough to contain all of life, all worship and work in prayer set in a structure adequate to the actual conditions in which it is lived out.' [2]

The new monasticism transcends both the Protestant and Roman Catholic monastic frameworks, which have dominated the Western Church since the Reformation. It is a discernment of shared rhythms; it is a recovery of normality. Some of the churches arising out of the sixteenth-century Protestant/Catholic schism have been dogmatically separatist. They have seen themselves as the centre of reform and have tended to look down on others. Monasticism, in contrast, is grounded in a humility that has no false or grandiose illusions. It has a deep connectedness, which derives from a recognition that there is only one holy, catholic, orthodox, apostolic church.

Post-modern Christians who seek a new monasticism are wary of structures that are imposed from the centre; they do not want to be trapped in a new legalism. They don't believe they should be shut off from ordinary people. They see themselves as on a journey, and can't pre-judge what they will be doing at a later stage of the journey. They want

2. Petersen, Eugene *The Belly of the Fish* (Eerdmans/Gracewing).

to be free to follow each prompting of the Spirit, to be single or to marry.

Planting people-friendly monastic churches that are born out of such a dynamic, and which do not have to be squeezed into a 'one-shape-fits-all' church structure, may be the only way to win them. For monasteries, whether old or new, are usually freed from the diocesan system so that they can develop under God according to their own prophetic charisms. This is recognised, in one way or another, in the regulations of the historic diocesan churches.[3]

It is interesting that St Thomas Church, Crookes, Sheffield is putting before the church authorities a proposal for a monastic order which can plant monastic-style mission churches in just such a framework, freed from parish and diocesan regulations.

The Cappadocian and other fathers of the Eastern Church did not treat fourth-century monasticism as a special form of Christian life, but as an actualisation of what in principle was a life demanded of all Christians.[4] The Celtic monastic churches were not regarded as a special

3. For example, the Advisory Council on the Relations of Bishops and Religious Communities in the Church of England states in *A Directory of the Religious Life* (1980): 'Religious communities are independent associations expressing by their life and work a prophetic role which complements, and sometimes challenges, the life of the church as a whole. They therefore need freedom from external control. Their status as independent bodies gives them complete and autonomous control of both their property and their internal government, in fulfilment of their spiritual vision. Yet the Church requires what both clergy and laity ask for: standards or norms by which religious communities can be guaranteed and recognised as in good standing.'

4. Greer, R. A. *Broken Lights and Mended Lives* (Pennsylvania State University Press, 1986).

form of church, they were the norm, for everybody could belong to them.

Eldred Willey, in his book *Prayers of New Communities* [5] introduces over twenty modern communities in the UK.

Brad Bessell, the founder of the Anamchara Community near Adelaide, is a young married person. He says, 'I know I am called to be a monk but I also have a heart for church planting.' He sees his home base, which he hopes will have enough land for others to live there, as the rural monastery, based on a daily rhythm of prayer and work. The Sunday church will be in the city, the mission outreach of the monastery. The Community of Aidan and Hilda's Way of Life is the basis of the church's life.

Monastic villages

In the USA two million people belong to mega-churches. These, though clothed in a much different culture, contain certain elements of the Celtic monastic city. The mega-church has food halls, sporting leagues, day care and learning groups as well as a variety of worship patterns. 'I am not the pastor of a church, I am the mayor of a city,' observed the leader of one mega-church. [6] The mega-churches lack, however, the spirituality of the monastic tradition, and they do not pray in the rhythms of creation. 'They have a limited shelf-life,' a TV commentator observed, 'because, like supermarkets, they have to follow the demographic curves.'

In Bergen, Norway, the 2400-member Pentecostal church also has certain elements of the monastic village. It

5. Willey, Eldred *Prayers of New Communities* (DLT, 2001).

6. BBC TV Newsnight, 2 January 2003.

has schools for children and adults and is starting its own bank. Every day over a hundred people gather for an hour's prayer meeting before going to work. But without cars this would disintegrate. Nobody lives there. It is not a spiritual home. Its members are living off a society that is dysfunctional; they are not creating an alternative economy.

In the gene pool of the Isles, however, is the memory of monastic villages spawning the first schools, hospitals, universities, libraries and even great towns. Many Celtic monastic churches had a real economy, which was viable, rooted in the neighbourhood and seen to benefit local people. It is, I believe, possible for us to reconnect with these roots and develop monastic villages on a smaller, more organic scale, using the networks of our technological society.

Pilgrim centres such as Iona, Lindisfarne and Taizé have elements of 'the monastic village' and draw many seekers. However, unlike the early monastic villages, whose various components grew out of the common wellspring of God's love, these places already have indigenous sub-communities, such as fishing, farming and tourism, with their own dynamics; the 'godly village' approach must be to respect these as they are, though holding out the possibility of voluntary transformation.

Many cathedral closes were once monastic villages, and some of these lend themselves to becoming so again. Yet in a book about cathedrals boldly entitled *Flagships of the Spirit*, in which various writers outlined uses for cathedrals, none had a plan for a cathedral to become a monastery. In one cathedral city three entities are within a stone's throw of each other: the cathedral, the diocesan office and the retreat house. Yet they neither pray, plan nor share their lives together. They are three competing businesses. Visitors are denied an experience of holistic, hospitable Christianity.

The absence of community in cathedral closes means that many tourists receive stones instead of bread.

Some cathedral closes lend themselves to becoming communities. The houses the Dean and Chapter rent out could be allocated to people who wish to follow a Rule of that Cathedral Community. Poor people who do not get married because they cannot afford the cost of a typical wedding could be invited to have picnic receptions in the cloisters. Even those that lack housing availability can do something, as has Bradford. Its Cathedral Centre is not a shop that sells postcards, but a drop-in, which offers food and friendship to the most needy.

A typical emerging monastic village might have more than one style of worship area, a café, an arts centre, workshops, guest accommodation, study and sports facilities, shops, playgroups, play area, a theatre or meeting hall, counselling and medical care, huts or *poustinias* for private study and contemplation, schools, family support, activities for the elderly, meditation rooms, organic fields or farm, peace garden and cyber facilities, all revolving around a daily rhythm of prayer, and a place of silence serviced by resident members who embrace common values and disciplines.

CHAPTER 9

Rise up! the Rainbow Church of the Isles

Islands are God's strategy for continents.
Conrad Hunte

At the turn of this millennium Britain's devolved Parliaments in Northern Ireland, Scotland and Wales joined the Republic of Ireland, the Channel Islands and the Isle of Man in a Council of the Isles.[1]

Could Northern Ireland become Europe's third such zone – a neutral region in a new Irish-British political dispensation, possibly to be followed by other intractable trouble spots, like Gibraltar and Cyprus?

1. The Council of the Isles is an informal name for 'The British-Irish Council' which was set up after the Good Friday Agreement in a treaty in March 1999. The Council comprises representatives of the British and Irish Governments, the devolved institutions in Scotland, Northern Ireland and Wales, and representatives from the Isle of Man and the Channel Islands. It aims 'to promote positive, practical relationships among the people of the islands, and to provide a forum for consultation and co-operation'. Europe already had such a fruitful model. The Nordic Council, comprising five nations and three autonomous regions, has been operating since 1952. It has effectively buried the territorial disputes which used to be endemic in the Scandinavian peninsula.

157

A major root of the conflict is the two mutually exclusive claims for sovereignty over one territory. In this sense, neither a United Kingdom nor a united Ireland is workable in the long term. Hence the timeliness of the two Governments renouncing their claims to unitary sovereignty, and agreeing to work towards a 'totality of relations'. Each unit would function with the appropriate degree of autonomy, with the council providing a co-ordinating and mediating role where necessary – for example, in managing fishery and pollution in the Irish Sea, a British-Irish electricity and gas connector, or inter-regional trade, tourism and cultural exchanges. It is worth noting that there are now probably as many people of Irish extraction living in Britain as there are in Ireland.

What is asked for is not a unilateral surrender, but rather a shifting of power – primarily *downwards* (as subsidiarity indicates) to regions and localities, but in some cases *upwards* to the transnational council.

This council – and the concept behind it – is an acorn that can grow into an oak. Whether it does or not may depend in part upon the churches of these lands. They have common roots and contain within themselves the power of possibility. The church is the soul of politics and the conscience of peoples. The vision of the church as a fellowship of faith communities engaged in healing their lands can connect with the populations in a way that the retreating church never did.

Defining the islands

Attempts to define Britain are littered with confusion. These are examined in Norman Davies' major history which, after other titles had to be rejected, he entitled *The*

Isles: A History.[2] Many histories of Britain confuse Britain with England, to the fury of Scots and Welsh, some of whom no longer want to be called British.

The *Oxford English Dictionary* defines 'Britain' as:

> The proper name of the whole island containing England, Wales, and Scotland, with their dependencies; more fully called Great Britain . . .

> The term 'British' can mean 'pertaining to the ancient Britons' or 'of or belonging to Great Britain, or its inhabitants'.

In a geographical sense the term 'British Isles' is still applied to Britain, Ireland and the smaller islands that skirt them, but in a political sense this is clearly not acceptable.

In the year 2000 Tony Blair's government thought corporate Britain needed to be rebranded, and the Home Secretary announced it was now 'Cool Britannia'. He announced it on April Fool's Day, however, and if it was trailing a kite, it had to be withdrawn. For one thing, it excluded Northern Ireland unionists, who were part of the 'United Kingdom of Great Britain and Northern Ireland'. So 'UK' became the Blair brand word. Yet neither the Channel Isles nor the Isle of Man are part of Britain or the United Kingdom; they are, however, linked through the Crown, and through defence and other treaties.

Some interesting facts and figures

Britain and Ireland

- Irish colonised parts of Britain before British colonised Ireland. The sixth-century Irish were known as Scotti, and the Irish kingdom of Dal Riada colonised a part of western Scotland and gave it the same name. They also

2. Norman Davies *The Isles: A History* (Macmillan, 1999).

gave their name to Scotland. Although Scots who legally purchased land in Northern Ireland at the behest of the British Government were regarded by the existing Irish population as part of a colonialist agenda, they came from stock which had some Irish origins.

- Citizens of the UK and of the Republic of Ireland can come and go and live as they please in each other's countries. A passport to one is a passport to the other.

- Ireland is only 14 miles from Britain at its nearest point, the Mull of Kintyre.

- Many Irish do not realise that their beloved St Patrick was a Briton, or that St Aidan, the apostle to the English, was Irish.

- The British are a mongrel people – Roman, Saxon, Scandinavian, Norman, Jewish, Afro-Caribbean, Asian – but before all of these we are Celtic. Christians in Celtic times united peoples from four hostile ethnic groups: the Gaels (mostly from Ireland), the Picts (mostly from Scotland), the Anglo-Saxons (mostly from England) and the ancient British (many from Wales). This offers hope to our multi-ethnic society.

- It is true that many, including Welsh and Scottish nationalists, do not like to be called British because they associate Britain with England. But historically the Britons were the people who lived here before the English (Anglo-Saxons) invaded. The word Welsh means British. So in this sense the Welsh and Scots are British, whatever political shape their countries take.

- Public figures such as the black broadcaster Trevor Phillips, urge people to think of themselves as Afro-Caribbean Britons, Asian Britons, English Britons, Irish Britons, Jewish Britons, Scottish Britons, Welsh Britons, etc.

- In a poll of 30,000 who voted for the people and items which summed up Britishness for the last 1000 years, only two out of a top list of 100 had a religious connection. These were Glastonbury and Stonehenge. The organised church was not perceived as endogynous, but at least two ancient religious places were. A renewal of our Celtic roots may well speak to the unchurched population in a way that our standardised banalities do not.

- Both Britain and Ireland are multi-ethnic not just as a result of recent waves of immigration, but in their origins. Two races, the 'aboriginals' who still survive in the Basques and in western Ireland and Britain, and the Celts, inhabited these islands at the time of the first century Roman conquest of Britain.

- The UK's Union Flag consists of three versions of the Christian Cross: St Andrew's (for Scotland), St George's (for England), and St Patrick's (for Ireland). The ban on Welsh people waving St David's flag (with its Cross) at Cardiff Arms Park instead of the Welsh dragon was withdrawn after recent uproar. Some people are calling for a British-Irish flag which incorporates St David's flag, a tinge of green and the inclusive Celtic circle.

- Historically, Ireland is comprised of the four kingdoms of Ulster, Connaught, Leinster and Munster (it was never unified except for a time under British rule). In myth, however, there is a fifth kingdom, variously named, which is on a higher, spiritual plain. We may name this Elysium. In myth Britain's King Arthur tried to unite warring kingdoms. He gathered great and good leaders to a round table where they planned how to turn Britain into a land of respect, chivalry and noble ideals. They, too, envisaged a kingdom which operated on a higher plane. We may name this Avalon.

The insight that two parties in an intractable dispute can meet in 'a third place' which is on a higher plain, lay behind the Irish Peace Process which began in the 1990s.

The Isle of Man

The term 'the island of Ireland' refers to the whole of the geographical entity. The 'Republic of Ireland' (formerly the 'Irish Free State' and then 'Eire') refers to the southern part of that island which became independent of Britain in 1922.

In the fifth century a revolution took place in Man. Saints such as Patrick, Germanus and Maughold planted the Christian faith there, and in the following two centuries Man was by blood and language closely linked with Ireland, which had then become a major seat of Latin learning in Europe. A remarkable number of keeills, or chapels, were built, and Man became known as 'the Holy Isle' (Ellan Shyiant). Its Parliament is independent.

The Channel Islands

The Channel Isles were evangelised by early saints such as Samson and were once dotted with hermitages. Guernsey was once known as the Holy Isle. They still retain elements of these praying communities. When the old French sisters decided to close their convent, Les Cotils, high above St Peter Port, Guernsey, people from local churches, conceiving a vision of it being 'a Galilee for Europe' managed to secure it. Local Christians staff its café, and the grounds now include a school and housing for the elderly. It sustains a daily pattern of prayer with or without guests.

The changing countries and their Churches

Britain, and its 401 associated islands, is still a vibrant state. This dynamism surely owes something to a love of liberty, a history of trading and a respect for Christian values. At the moment its role in Europe and the world is under review, and internal tensions have come to the surface. Devolved Parliaments in Northern Ireland, Scotland and Wales demand a refashioning of political structures and regional identities. Protestantism, such an essential feature of British identity since the Reformation, is losing its monopoly. The multi-ethnic make-up of most big cities challenges traditional culture.

The Empire gave Britain a purpose: to bring civilisation to the world. It now lacks a moral vision. Fighting for human rights is good, but this on its own lacks a sense of society. We have lost the sense of the sacred and the holistic view of things that goes with that, also a sense of morality, even the idea of truth itself. There is a fragmentation of conscience. Government wants contradictory things at the same time – for example, a neutral state and family values. Uncertain of their philosophies, political parties swing with popular opinion.

Freedom needs a moral framework for its own survival. We are losing the capacity to distinguish the essential from the trivial. With a rediscovery of the Divine Presence in the individual and society will come a true appraisal of ourselves and a sense of what God can do through us. Such knowledge could transform us.[3]

Much of the above three paragraphs are inspired by an article by my friend Philip Boobyer.

3. *Daily Mail*, 13 September 1999.

Our future identity will depend upon discovering this vision of the Presence in all things; it will also depend upon how we choose to remember the past – being honest about the bad but also celebrating good aspects: liberty without decadence, trade without exploitation, faith which brings care.

The Church, if it lives out its divine intention, is the engine for this revolution. The Church is the conscience of the nation, the source of its wisdom, the motivator of its people, the spiritual home that enables peoples of many ethnic backgrounds to relate as one family. For churches comprise people who are brothers and sisters with stronger ties than those which divide along ethnic lines.

A survey into national identity published in 1999 found that the English are an insecure people who are increasingly reviled by their proud Celtic neighbours, and even by the Cornish and Northern populations within England. While devolved Scotland, Wales and Northern Ireland were emerging as confident nations, the English had an identity crisis. Fiona Gilmore, the managing director of Springpoint, said the crisis of Englishness 'was a thread that ran throughout the 77-page report' and that she was amazed by its strength.[4]

Dominant symbols of the English, according to this survey, were lager louts, soccer hooligans, strawberries and fish and chips. Jeremy Paxman, in his book *The English: a Portrait of a People* (Michael Joseph 1999) asked whether the old English, polite people with hot-water bottles who dominated an Empire, any longer have a place. He recognised the English are in crisis. They cut themselves off from Europe in the sixteenth century, they lost an Empire in the

4. *UK – Voices of Our Times*, Springpoint, 31 Corsica Street, London N5 1JT.

twentieth century and, quoting the English church historian David Edwards, they 'have lost any sense of what religion is'. Paxman felt that a new English nationalism is possible – less likely to be based on flags and anthems, than in the green of England. With strong spiritual roots, its marks are stability without froth; humour; the ability to hold together different things.

Entrepreneurs are in their element, and small, entrepreneurial churches are emerging, each with an individuality, a workshop here, a project there. The Church of England can be part of this if its bishops move from regulation to relationship; and if its grass roots get on with entrepreneurial experiments, trusting that in due course bishops will bless rather than exclude them.

The prosperity of the Irish Republic within the European Union means it is a confident, equal partner with Britain and the Roman Catholic Church is losing its monopoly as protector.

Increasingly the churches of the third millennium will have national characteristics more than denominational. This way of being church was there from its beginning. In the Letters to the Seven Churches (Revelation, Chapters 1-3) each church reflects a particular characteristic of its region. Vatican Two documents distinguish between what belongs to the local and what belongs to the universal Church.

This vision of a Church of the Isles can only ripen to its fullness if the Churches rediscover the roots they have in common. Contrary to some expectations, a recovery of roots will also connect with the general population.

The third millennium began with Churches Together in Britain holding a major act of worship, with a member of Britain's Royal family present at each, in the capital cities of England, Northern Ireland, Scotland and Wales.

Churches Together may do this century what the Celtic churches did in the seventh century, provide the uniting fellowship that bonds together Britain's unity in diversity. But that, great though it is, is not all.

The creation of Churches Together in Britain and Ireland in the 1980s has led to a friendlier relationship between the churches. Independent evangelical churches, which, in older days, would have boycotted other churches now, in some areas, have a humbler attitude and are willing to work in partnership.

Rise up! a Rainbow Church of the Isles

The story of Jesus raising Lazarus, bound in stinking grave clothes, from the tomb of death (John 11) is a parable for today's Church. Those who are concerned for the Church are like Lazarus' sisters, Martha and Mary, weeping at the tomb and asking the Lord why he has not done something; fretting, perhaps angry or fearful.

Jesus knows what is going on, he is 'on the case'! Some people wanted Jesus to come earlier, before the full extent of the death process had set in. But Jesus wanted him to stay dead. He was not interested in a partial or piecemeal recovery. The signs that Jesus had something in mind was the rolling away of the stone that covered the grave, and the unrolling of the grave clothes that bound him. There are large stones that shut in the Church and decaying clothes that we thought were necessary but which we must now divest ourselves of. As we do this, and we wait for God's timing, then, as in Ezekiel's vision of a people of dry bones, Christ will resurrect his Body in our lands.

In Ireland

In Ireland, the overlaying of the homely intimacy with God and the saints which marked its first Christian centuries must be rolled away. Perhaps the clothes that bind the Body are priests on pedestals, prayer fossilised in ritual, and the stereotyping of other branches of Christ's Church.

A Roman Catholic from Ireland was present at *The Roots for Renewal* symposium which launched the Community of Aidan and Hilda, at which modern liturgies in the Celtic style were used. 'These are what the church in Ireland needs' he told us. 'The naturalness of Irish spirituality has been overlaid by a liturgy which is unnatural. This way of worship allows people to be familiar with their own saints.'[5]

In Ireland, despite the pride and prejudice of centuries which makes this seem unlikely, there is a trend which indicates how an unforced coming together is possible. The renewal of Christian Celtic roots, which in the past Protestants thought belonged to 'the other side', is now beginning to be owned also by them. The Orange Lodge published a book on Patrick which enabled them to own him. Presbyterian and Methodist ministers have corresponded with me about how they can renew their Celtic roots, and face up to the fact that the Reformation was not perfect.

The Irish Peace Process was accompanied by an unheralded but deep process of spiritual healing. At one gathering a prophetic picture was given of a man who raped a woman and had a bastard child. The bastard child was Ulster. An Ulster Protestant was moved to tearfully embrace a buxom Catholic from the South and call her 'Mama'.

The emerging Ireland is becoming less tribal, more diverse, open, prosperous and also rejecting the unacceptable

5. These are included in Simpson, Ray *Celtic Worship Through the Year* (Hodder & Stoughton 1997) and are subsumed in the more comprehensive four volumes of *The Celtic Prayer Book* published by Kevin Mayhew.

face of clericalism. The renewal of Celtic spirituality offers a way for the Irish who love God, but who are offended by all this, to go on journeys, be hospitable and to let the fire blaze in places of prayer.

In Wales

Wales is a small country of some three million souls, 20 per cent of whom speak Welsh, mostly as their mother tongue. Twelve per cent are members of a Christian church: 150,000 are Roman Catholics, 100,000 are Church in Wales members, and the remaining churches make up the other 200,000 members. The people of Wales know that their culture was formed when Christianity penetrated its life and being in the years 400-800 after Christ.

> The dust of all the saints and martyrs
> of the ages rest in your lap.
>
> *Gwenallt 1899-1968*

The 'stone' which has kept Christ's Body entombed consists in large measure of English domination. For most of Wales' history this has belittled its character and spirituality. The Act of Union between England and Wales in 1536 replaced the Latin of the established Church's public worship, not with Welsh, but with English. This alienated the people. In the seventeenth century many new Nonconformist chapels and Anglican churches worshipped God in Welsh. Welsh became the language of religion and this 'saved its standards and provided an unbroken theme in the history of Wales down to our very day.[6] In the eighteenth century, revival swept Wales. In 1920 the Church in Wales came into being, and lost its funding from the Church of England. Yet church

6. Jones J. *This Land and People: A Simposium on Christian and Welsh National Identity*, ed. P. H. Ballard and D. H. Jones (University College, Cardiff, 1979) p. 18.

and chapel were divided among themselves. The land is now littered with derelict chapels and churches which signal the steep decline in churchgoing. The National Eisteddford has kept alive the Welsh spirit, but precious little else has.

> There is widespread disillusionment within the churches with the Church itself . . .
>
> We are in danger of being imprisoned by a spirituality of decline.
>
> *Noel Davies, General Secretary, Churches Together in Wales*

However, speaking back in 1917 at the Convention of the Church in Wales, the Lord Justice Bankes said: 'I see in my mind's eye a truly national Church, a Church that will adapt itself to the needs and requirements of all classes and to the ever-changing conditions under which her work must be done, a Church whose sympathy, whose toleration, whose enthusiasm will draw all people to her and enshrine herself permanently in the affections of the inhabitants of Wales.'

> The stinking grave clothes that must now be removed may be the sectarian spirit. *The challenge of gospel and culture in Wales today is the challenge to recover catholicity, to recover wholeness.*
>
> *Noel Davies*

After years of decline where disunity and dogma have ruled, are there signs of new moves of God? In 1995 a leader in one of the new Churches took back to Wales a powerful prophecy: Pay heed to your genetic code. Wales' National Assembly, despite initial misgivings, has brought some increase in Welsh pride and possibility. There is an increasing thirst for unity in Wales. Prophet voices speak of a rediscovery of the underground stream running through Wales, interpreted as the Revivals and the first stream of faith in Wales' 'age of the saints'; of a church of creativity, reaching the needy, yet a church also for the business and political community; a church finding favour with Social Services and the like, a church reaching out and resourcing Wales and the Nations. There was a sense that the Charismatic and House Church movements had largely achieved their aims, and now was the time for something new. Church members were encouraged to sense in their hearts the things that could only be seen dimly at the moment.

The retreating churches are putting up walls. The emerging churches are places of hospitality, retreat and healing. The healing centre at the newly restored ancient shrine of Pennant-Melangell, the community and retreat house at Coleg y Groes, the multi-faceted United Reformed Church at Llanfair Penrhos, the provision of prayer rooms in the grounds of traditional faith communities, are signs of these new shoots.

English dominance is being removed by membership of the European Union and changed attitudes towards colonialism. The sense of worthlessness that English colonialism induced in many Welsh people Jesus intends now to heal. Jesus' message is still: 'I no longer call you servants; you are my friends if you do what I tell you.' Healed churches seek to connect, not with the church cultures that are obsolete but with the whole that has been lost, with the deeper current of God's Presence.

In Scotland

'Most of the Church in Scotland is in denial' says a leading church figure. A church that does not realise anything is wrong cannot be helped. Before Jesus got Lazarus unbound his sisters wept. The church people of Scotland need to learn to weep. Shortly after the nation-moving funeral of Diana, Princess of Wales, I led a workshop on 'lament' for some Scottish churches. An elderly, life-long church-goer prayed: 'Lord, please forgive us that all these years in church we've locked up our feelings and not shared them with you.' The stone that emtombs Christ's Body in Scotland is the mindset that treats the Reformation as an end road rather than as a launching pad. The wretched clothes that bind the Body so tightly are the spirit of control.

This spawns fear of charismatic gifts, creative arts, church planting outside inherited structures and other church traditions.

Scotland's two largest churches, the Roman Catholic and the Presbyterian Church of Scotland, are losing members, but the folk memory of Catholic versus Protestant is flourishing, as may be witnessed at Glasgow's two tribal football teams of Celtic and Rangers. Healing can come if the deep Presbyterian-Catholic divide in Scotland is looked at in terms of temperament as well as history.

Inter-church partnership is growing, but Church of Scotland minister Andrew Dick says, 'We have to build the nests before we lay the eggs.' In his parish of Musselburgh, because the celebrations hosted by the churches together are growing, the means for regular prayer and planning are needed. A 'nest' may prove to be the most helpful way of evolving.

New churches, like the Musselburgh Fellowship, with their flexibility, may take the lead in establishing the Celtic-style communities or 'nests' that Scotland needs. 'The Raven', a kind of experimental 'Clubland Monastery' in Edinburgh was initiated by the parish founded by St Cuthbert in the seventh century, surely a sign that death and resurrection are possible.

The Church of Scotland's vision of 'A Church without Walls'[7] can enable networking across the traditional divides, and connect up with the current of civil renewal generated by Scotland's new parliament.

In England

The stone that covers up Christ's Body in England may be materialism. The population feeds on material things and on the glitter of passing fashion, fame and fortune. And perhaps the grave clothes that bind consist of 'the light half-belief in casual creeds', the myth that anything may be believed by anyone without consequences.

In the light of the old adage 'If you stand for nothing you fall for anything' it is not surprising that English people have surfeited themselves with the surface pleasures of the global village. 'The new England is Buddhism, aromatherapy, French wines and line dancing,' concluded Darcus Howe, the former Black Panther, in his celebrated TV series *The White Tribe*. He could find nothing distinctively English.

Yet did he and others look in the right places? The *Lion Heart* is the magazine of a new church in Alnwick, Northumberland, where a member told me that God is doing a new thing. He is calling the roast-beef people of England to love him with all their hearts and minds, in a way that is natural to them, and the Church is the people doing that.

In this England, individuality flowers, because it is rooted in the green and solid earth, and the land itself is being healed. Oaks are a sign of this rootedness. Oaklings are springing up, which will be the oaks of the future. The contribution of recent immigrants to church life is enormous.

7. See the Church of Scotland's website www.churchwithoutwalls.org.uk

The decline in church-going has been stemmed in London because so many immigrants have joined and are helping to sustain the churches.

In all the Isles

The second millennium forms of Church, shaped firstly by political power games, secondly by denominational truth claims, and only thirdly by Christ's love, are fading, leaving a large vacuum. For the first time since the Celtic Mission a majority of the population has no contact with any church.

Yet Christianity itself is not dying. New Christian networks multiply. A hopeful example of these is the TwentyFourSeven and the Boiler House movements. Young Christians from all Church streams form in rotation temporary 'monasteries' – places of continuous and creative prayer.

Between such new shoots and our early Celtic roots lie the dying denominational frameworks. How can the shoots, the roots and the old growths relate to one another in a way that brings sustaining life for all?

A shared vision of the emergence, in varied forms, of 'villages of God' can enable this. Just as certain cities designate areas as zones for this or that (green, smoke-free, nuclear-free, fair trade for example), so churches together can designate certain areas as villages of God. A village of God may include places of prayer, education, counsel, art, silence, and leisure. In these, churches will not compete, they will complete. A Catholic care home for lone mothers, a Salvation Army soup kitchen, an Anglican meditation centre and a New Church arts and youth centre can each be true to themselves and yet be part of one villlage. There could even be a synagogue, mosque or temple which, though independent, share a common eating place with the Christians.

Over the year different ethnic groups would host distinctive seasonal celebrations to which all are invited.

Some villages of God would develop their own shops, health or school facilities. Smaller ones would relate to such facilities that already exist in such a way that, like the yeast that transforms dough, these facilities begin to reflect something of the ethos of the village of God.

Villages of God are growing out of hub churches, pilgrimage centres and co-operative church ventures and some will consist of networks of association and technology.

As this new framework for the Church of the Isles catches on, churches and groups in many places will 'map' their areas in prayer, identify existing resources, embrace these as potential parts of a village of God, and establish resource centres that are lacking in the area. These can be physically linked by inspired walkways, information plaques, 'village of God trail leaflets' and common websites. These will be 'people's villages', not because they are formally democratic, but because all can feel at home. They are places where people can be in touch with their emotions, cry, pray or chill out. They are secure places because they are rooted in God.

They will also be linked across the seas. The Irish hatred of England has been caused by British misdeeds, not by instinctive hostility. If the English can truly make restitution and the Irish can truly release today's Britain from its condemnation, something instinctive will emerge. Instinctively, the British like the Irish; and the Irish are as big hearted as any people on earth.

Freelance editor and writer Clive Price writes:

> As an Englishman, to become connected to the people and the land of Ireland – even in my own humble way – is a special experience, as if I am running on two cultural and

spiritual cylinders – England and Ireland – rather than just one. My mind and spirit have been freshly inspired.

There is a deep spiritual well under the surface of Ireland. Having discovered that intuitively, now I am investigating that intellectually – and becoming even more deeply moved by the wonder of it all. What we need is a bond across our nations, and maybe this is happening at a level that goes beyond political treaties, important though they are. It's a treaty of the heart – and it can start with just some of us, building up friendships across the Irish Sea.

The Churches of the Isles are meant to meet, not so much in formal synods as in fellowship, fests and waitings upon God. This is a great hope. The old demarcations of denominations will become less rigid as fellowship grows between Churches within these lands.

A rainbow people of God is emerging, willy-nilly. A rainbow embraces all the colours (all the elements) yet you cannot capture or compartmentalise it. The original rainbow which followed the flood from which God saves Noah and the animals was a sign. It was a sign of God's commitment to his believing people and to his earth. The new Rainbow Church heals the land.

There is a place in this Rainbow Church of the Isles for people of every ethnic and ecclesial background, for new Christians who have not joined a local church and for non-believing neighbours who want to be friends. There is room for every kind of creative impulse to be explored, for styles of worship and prayer that fit every temperament. This is a vision, a possibility and a call to which it is worth giving the flower of our lives.

The rainbow which was the stuff of dreams becomes the over-arching glory of our lands.

Study Guide
Celtic Models for Modern Churches

Twelve sessions on developing
people-friendly congregations

Course contents

We are now entering one of the greatest watershed periods in human history. Creation itself is charged with the electricity of these times and is beginning to groan and travail for what is about to come . . . In preparation for this greatest of events the Church is about to go through a metamorphosis. She is going to change from a worm into a butterfly. A caterpillar is confined to the earth, and its path must conform to the contour of the earth. Likewise, for nearly two thousand years the Church has often conformed more to the ways of the world than to the ways of the Spirit.

Soon the Church will go through a change so dramatic, she will seem to emerge as an entirely different creature. It will be like another birth . . .

Rick Joyner, The Morning Star Prophetic Bulletin

INTRODUCTION

Who is this course for?

An existing or specially convened church group, which reports back to the church leadership, which hopefully sets up a task group to put insights into action. Ecumenical and embryo church groups may also profit from it.

The aims of the course

To identify:

- the changing social framework in which the church is set
- the unhelpful anachronisms it must discard
- the neglected scriptural essentials it needs to bring into focus

To draw insight from Celtic and contemporary Churches

To suggest some practical steps forward.

Length

The course is designed to last one term of 12 weeks, though it may meet less often over a longer period. There are two optional extra sessions on values and leadership.

Attitude

The group should cherish the church as Christ cherishes his own body (Ephesians 5:29). This requires honesty about what is wrong, but not a dismissive approach.

181

Format

Most sessions should include:

- prayer
- Bible study
- meditation or focusing
- teaching
- discussion
- a practical appraisal or exercise
- worship and dedication.

This is not detailed in the session notes. The group leader needs to plan this beforehand.

Style

Since church styles vary, this will range from the informal to the formal. The style should be what makes members feel comfortable. We have therefore made no suggestions for worship, but the leaders need to prepare this. Some groups will want to include refreshments before or after the session.

Leaders

It is best if there is a leader and a co-leader or facilitator. If possible the leaders should pray and plan together before the group meetings.

Getting started

In churches with groups that are already motivated, the church leaders simply need to talk through the course with the group leaders and announce it. If this is to be a new group, the church leaders need to take time to explain the relevance of the course and to build up expectation. They need to decide who should be in the group. For example, it could be an existing leaders' team/council, etc. or it could be for any church member.

Preparatory meeting

If it is a new group, prospective members might find it helpful to meet briefly after a church service to have it explained and to sign up. At this meeting the church leader should:

- outline the course, times, dates, venue;
- outline the aims and attitudes mentioned in the Introduction;
- introduce the group leaders.

Follow up

If the church appoints a task group, the group leaders should provide them with feedback or proposals from the study group. If the church has no task group, or if the study group is ecumenical, leaders should try to feed back to the churches' leaders.

Some material in this Study Guide first appeared in various incarnations of my book *The Spiritual Renewal of a Neighbourhood*. This was first published by the Diocese of Norwich Training Team as a course workbook. The Church Army published it in revised form as a workbook plus a handbook for course leaders. These are now out of print.

SESSION 1

The Big Culture Shift

Humanity is going through a massive shift in its mental framework. As a result, the model of Church that has withstood the ravages of centuries seems near the end of its shelf life.

> The traces of Constantine's Church would seem to be fading, and a turning point as fundamental as the Constantinian one confronts us.
>
> *Cardinal Franz König*

Living Churches heed Jesus' advice to understand the context of their time – you can tell the season by looking at the trees (Mark 13:28-29).

Jesus gave a warning. Read Luke 5:36.

Jesus told us it is no good trying to tear off a bit of new cloth and sew it onto the old. The mental framework of the emerging society can be likened to new cloth. The old framework is like old cloth. We cannot expect people who are seeking a spirituality in the new framework to find it in churches that are wedded to the old framework. The big decline in churchgoing is a warning. We have to weave new cloth.

An example of this is Andrew, a spiritual seeker: 'I wanted to find a path. In the church I found only ritual.' Think of other examples.

> This is an age in which the cloth is being unwoven.
> It is therefore no good trying to patch.
> We must rather set up the loom on which coming generations
> may weave new cloth according to the pattern God provides.
>
> *Mother Mary Clare*, Oxford

In order to 'weave the new cloth' we need to distinguish between the divine essence of the church: the rich, living tradition which is God's gift on the one hand, and the now dead man-made traditions, the accretions of fallen human nature, that mar it.

The Church, when it is true to its Head, is eternally old and eternally new. It relates to all that has flowed from its Head since its inception with reverence. What is new is the way it relates this to the present.

Its essence is the message, morality and living spirit of Jesus in his followers, ministers and sacraments. The gates of hell shall not ultimately prevail against the church (Matthew 16:18). We need to cherish the heart of the church through perpetual prayer.

But there is no doubt that any particular form of church can perish. The travel writer William Dalrymple describes in his book *From The Holy Mountain* how churches in Turkey, which have survived many trials since the first Christian century, are now in their last decade on earth.

What is the new culture frame?

The Enlightenment culture split different parts of life into compartments. It separated:

• reason from faith,

- body from soul,
- sacred from secular,
- masculine from feminine,
- earth from spirit,
- science from religion,
- work from prayer,
- organisation from values.

Give other examples.

The emerging culture is holistic. Some examples are:

- The concept of the biosphere views the world as a living, interrelated organism.
- The Green movement views humans and earth as partners in the web of life.
- New technology enables us to replace hierarchy with networking, and standardised ways with personalised service.
- Feminism balances left-brained, male, cerebral domination with intuitive, creative partnership.
- Post-modern people mistrust dogma and trust whatever feels good.

If you do not understand any of these, ask a question.

Things the Church needs to discard

Third-millennium churches need to relate to the third-millennium framework or they will become dinosaurs.

It is a good instinct to draw people into the church by removing barriers. The barriers we should remove are practices, mind-sets and structures that do not mirror Christ and his Body. (We should not remove the message, morality or living spirit of Jesus because the selfish egos of people resist them, for these are boundaries God gives for the benefit of all people.)

Read John 12:24. A precondition of renewal, in both nature and spiritual life, is the ability to 'die'. This applies to any one form of church.

Here are some things various church groups think the church should discard. Write this on a flipchart:

- Locked church buildings
- Belittling women, minorities or people of other faiths
- Being defined (e.g. RC or Protestant) by a sixteenth-century protest movement
- Bureaucratic denominational structures
- 'We know best' attitude
- Wordy, status-conscious and pontificating ways
- Unnatural programmes and jargon
- Wordy and packaged worship

Add to this list.

Bible Study

A Bible episode which illustrates the difference between godly and ungodly barriers is in John 8:2-11. Read this . . . The Pharisees had prejudice towards someone, who in this case was a prostitute. Jesus loved her so much that he showed by his loving tones, his absence of condemnation and his presence that he did not wish to reject her. He removed the barrier of prejudice. However, he required her to sin no more by ceasing to have sex outside a marriage relationship. He did not remove moral norms; he did remove cultural antagonism.

Meditate silently on this passage and then add to the list of alienating practices that your church needs to discard.

Some reasons why we need new models of Church

1. Two decades ago the book *Megatrends* predicted that as society grew more technological, people would seek more natural and supernatural experience to restore balance to a plastic world. It also predicted people would be drawn to the past.

   In the West there is a falling away from churches. Spiritual thirst draws many towards earth-based spiritualities. Because Celtic Christianity grew in the ferment of a nature religion it retained a soul-deep appreciation of the earth, whereas other expressions of Christianity dismissed the material world as fallen and therefore as worthless.

2. Generation X is fed up with fragmented Christianity. Christians no longer want to be defined by a protest movement four hundred years ago (the Reformation). In Celtic Christianity the great Christian streams flow together as one.

3. Many people now yearn for the mystical. This change in what people seek has reached deep even into the young Evangelical world. According to Wheaton College professor Gary Burge: 'Say "liturgy" and my evangelical students have a reflex action akin to an invitation to do a quiz; say "mysticism" and they are drawn, fascinated, eager to see what I mean . . .'

4. Many Protestant Churches dismissed the arts as worldly. Celtic Christianity uses the arts in order to be holy (whole). The prolific artistic, mystical and literary monks of Ireland may encourage life-denying Christians to embrace artistic expression as worship of the First Creator.

5. Sunday-only congregations who are separated from everyday life fail to meet people's need for a complete way of life.

Suggest other reasons why we need fresh models of church.

In the closing time of worship, express sorrow for the things the church must discard, and ask forgiveness.

Task group

Arrange for the church to dedicate a period (e.g. Lent or a special week) to confessing wrong attitudes or habits. Record these. Hold a service of releasing and receiving. This may use these words: 'Lord, we release to you this wrong attitude . . . Lord, we receive from you this new grace . . .'

A New Way of Being Church

> Systems, projects, meetings – that is church. Lord, how I long for church to be family, presence, meeting.
>
> *A church member*

Many of the historic Churches have a parish system.

> We are coming to the end of the parish phase of church.
>
> *Bishop Ian Harland*

In the second millennium Roman Catholic and Reformed Churches reflected the Imperial Civil Service model of the Roman Empire. Even new and missionary Churches adopted the top-down, 'one shape fits all' model.

Now many Churches are collapsing. Is this because they reflect patterns that are alien to most people today?

A modern parable

A new university received its first intake of students before the paths had been laid. So its wise planners observed the tracks students made across flowerbeds and laid the paths along those tracks.

The moral

Where modern people bypass our churches we have to observe the tracks they make (e.g. networks and meeting places such as shopping malls and leisure centres) and plant churches along those lines. For there is no evidence that spiritual quest has decreased.

To do

Give other examples of these modern non-church 'tracks'. Spiritual seekers are also drawn to some types of church, e.g:

- Churches in houses (cells or groups)
- 'Hub churches' (large umbrella congregations, pilgrim centres)
- Churches which have shared values and a heart for the people of the area
- Those with 'spaces' for people of different temperaments.

To do

Add to this list.

Objection

'Surely there is only one proper way of being church. It is sacrilege to let go of this.'

'The House that John Built'

In fact an alternative to the imperial way of being church was modelled in Eastern and Celtic lands in early centuries. It has been described as 'The House that John Built' because John, perhaps more than any other apostle, modelled church as a large household of love. He wrote letters to seven churches inspired by a vision of the Risen Christ (Revelation, Chapters 2-3) and discipled faith communities in the area now known as Turkey, some of whose leaders, such as Bishop Irenaeus, came to Gaul.

Celtic churches felt a rapport with John, and with alternative churches that grew up in the deserts, because these were based less on regulation (as in the Latin part of the Roman Empire) and more on relationship, and intimacy with God. At their heart was a holiness that freed people to be themselves.

From the sixth century the Irish churches were people's monasteries, which turned Ireland into 'a land of saints and scholars'. These were then exported to the English.

1. People's monastery churches served as prayer base, drop-in centre, library, school, health centre. They offered soul friends, training, entertainment and work to local people. Visitors brought the news of the world. They were completely open to the world. They were not enclosed, as were continental monasteries, which had the 'us and them' mentality that Protestants later rejected. In Celtic monasteries children, housewives, farm workers and visitors would wander in and out and worship together.

Discuss

In what ways can we become natural centres that draw all people of goodwill? *(7 minutes)*

2. The major Celtic monasteries were built on the main highways of sea and river in order to penetrate the population. Others grew, unplanned, out of places of spiritual retreat. There is need for both types of church today.

3. There was diversity – each monastery church had its own flavour in worship and values (Rule) yet each was connected with the whole church through common practices such as prayer, fasting, forgiveness, giving to the poor, keeping the Christian festivals, pilgrimaging to the world Christian centres and priests ordained in the apostolic succession.

4. Celtic monastic church buildings were expendable and expandable. They consisted of wooden huts and meeting places, which could easily be dismantled or added to. Name ways in which modern churches that have outgrown their first building have expanded. *(2 minutes)*

5. Irish churches introduced reading and writing to the people. Many druids and bards received this new gift of learning with open arms. Christianity had something to give, which the people wanted. Do we have anything to give, which the people want? *(3 minutes)*

6. Members of these churches regarded their founders as spiritual fathers or mothers whose authority lay in the mutual obligations of love. Yet they continued to have bishops living with them who were consecrated by bishops from the wider church. How can your local church best express this principle of home-grown leaders and a link with wider church leadership? *(5 minutes)*

Bible Study

Read 1 Timothy 3:15. Why do you think Paul described the church as a household?

Read John 15:1-16. Fruit is that which is produced naturally from us being what we are. That which rises to the surface is that which arises from our rootedness in Christ. Success is to be measured by being who we are – made in God's likeness. Churches are to be communities in which we can be who we are.

The shape of the Church – from squares to circles

The church has to have a structure, or shape.

The square has been used as a symbol for the second-millennium top-down, territorial church, which defines itself by external boundaries.

The circle has been used as a symbol of the third-millennium church, which defines itself by the Presence of God in life's natural patterns.

Brainstorm

Place a square on one sheet and a circle on another sheet of paper. Fill these in with words that describe what the square church and what the circle church of the future might be like.

Task group

Discern how your church can become less like a square and more like a circle, and act upon what you discern.

SESSION 3

A Journeying People

Post-modern people dislike rigid boundaries. To travel is more important than to arrive.

We should frequently recall that the leader of our church is Jesus Christ, who called himself 'the way' (John 14:6). If our leader is 'the way' the church must be more like a tent than a terminus.

Bible Study

In the Acts of the Apostles people nicknamed church members 'the Way' (e.g. Acts 9:1-2). The church, reflecting its members, gave the impression of being on a journey, on a voyage of discovery with God. Over the centuries the church has accumulated buildings, structures and mind-sets which focus on maintaining what it has, rather than on moving on with God.

Discuss

What nickname might non-churchgoers give to churches today? *(3 minutes)*

The primary model for the Old Testament 'church' was the people-on-the-move with God. They allowed God to show them through creation when to move and when to stay put.

Read Exodus 13:20-22 and briefly share any thoughts that strike you.

Later, when they were settled, they recalled God's way of leading them when they faced a new challenge. Moses speaks to the people of God about their fear of a hostile group who were bigger than them.

Read Deuteronomy 1:29-33 and briefly share any thoughts that strike you.

In Celtic society

Celtic churches were anchored but they were not stuck in an outdated mould. They cherished what they had received but that made them responsive to the Spirit who permeated their environment.

- Prayer and listening to God was built into their routine patterns.
- They released members as the Spirit moved them to travel as pilgrims.
- When numbers grew they moved into small, easy-to-dismantle buildings; they were not empire builders.
- They gave away rather than accumulated possessions.
- They told stories and meditated on great voyagers of faith such as Brendan the Navigator.
- They went on pilgrimages in order to act out God's call to journey.

Kevin was a tall, attractive young man who dressed in skins and walked long distances. He travelled to the edges of life in order to meet God there, and was led to live in a cave at

Glendalough. Over the years many were drawn to live and worship nearby. The 'monastic city' of Glendalough emerged. No doubt the example of their founder inspired them to 'live simply and travel lightly'. They refused to build a large, cathedral-type church; they just built small churches as needed. If you travel to Glendalough, some 20 miles from Dublin, you can visit the remains of these seven churches.

Examples of churches on a journey

1. Brother Roger, prior of the French community church at Taizé, refused the gift of a house because, he said, 'it makes everything so complicated'. His church is committed to 'the pilgrimage of trust on earth'. Even their worship building can expand or contract according to changing numbers.

2. A congregation in Sunderland gave its large building to local groups who serve the neighbourhood, and divided itself into eight sections, which met in smaller venues.

3. A visitor to Lindisfarne shared a vision of a Travelling Church across North America of two million people.

Exercise

Describe an existing (or, if this is not possible, an imaginary) church that models some aspect of journey for you.

Ways for churches to get moving

Cityside Church, Auckland, New Zealand asked each member to return a form with their answers to these questions:

1) One thing you've found helpful
2) One thing you've found unhelpful
3) One thing you'd like to see.

The responses were photocopied and put on the church website for all to see.

- Studley church has introduced listening and sharing services once a month.
- A church in Norwich asked each group in the church to draw up targets for the coming year and to decide what activities had run their course and should cease.
- Some churches appoint a person to record the story of God's hand in their history, or they appoint a group, or a wise outside person, to help them discern where God has led and is leading them.
- One church council begins every meeting with a time of silent waiting upon God, and allows their agenda to be shaped by it.
- Some churches listen to their neighbourhood and draw up an agenda based on what local people perceive their deepest needs to be.

What's to be done if we feel stuck inside the old system?

- Discern what God is wanting to bring about and co-operate with it.
- Discern what God is wanting to end and leave it – but with love.

Exercises

1. Moving on in the little things

Divide into fours. Have a time of silent listening. Then share a) which things in the church group, meeting or service in which you are involved have run their course and should be ended, and b) what new step should be taken.

2. Moving on in the bigger things

Repeat as before. Then share what clutter the church as a whole needs to leave behind, and what it needs to open its heart to.

Task group

Make a display, pamphlet or video of your church's journey since it began, highlighting God's hand in it.

Hold a listening day and highlight where you believe the church should go now.

SESSION 4

Friends of the Earth

The key issue

> I stopped going to churches because they did not honour
> the earth. I stopped going to New Age communities
> because they did not honour Christ. Where can I find a
> church that honours both the earth and Christ?
>
> *Judith*

> My church teaches me to be reconciled to God and to
> people, but it does not teach me to be reconciled to the
> earth.
>
> *Catherine*

Ecological awareness is on the increase. Respected experts
believe that the earth in its present form will not survive
unless the fast-expanding human race radically changes
longstanding selfish habits. People who seek the good of
the earth seek something that God desires, yet few of these
perceive churches to be allies. Many of these people recognise
that to befriend the earth requires spirituality, yet few of them
find creation-friendly spirituality in the churches. Many
people seek a spirituality that is natural, and they feel violated
if the church puts on unnatural airs or neglects the earth.

To be creation-friendly does not mean that we don't take sin or Jesus seriously. The Bible teaches us to be creation-friendly.

Bible Study

Read John 1:1. In the Greek language in which this was written 'Word' is 'Logos', which can also be translated as 'Life-force'.

Read Colossians 1:16-17. Discuss how you understand the phrase 'all things hold together in Christ'.

The Bible's record of God's saving acts is set in the framework of God creating everything (Genesis 1 and 2). God named the first man Earth (Adamah). Mr Earth's first act was to name, and thereby bless, each of earth's creatures (Genesis 2:19). Jesus Christ, whom St Paul names 'the second Adam' meaning 'the second Mr Earth' (1 Corinthians 15:47) comes from heaven, yet contains within his humanity the whole evolving earth story, and its groaning in anticipation of its coming total fulfilment (Romans 8:19-23).

In early and Celtic churches

Maximus the Confessor (d. 662) taught that the Creator-Logos has implanted in each created thing a characteristic 'thought', which is God's presence, and which makes it distinctively itself and at the same time draws it towards God. By virtue of this indwelling logos each created thing is not just an object but a personal word addressed to us by the Creator.

This creation-friendly theology continues to this day in the Eastern Church but in western churches an earth-denying theology took over. Spirit was divorced from matter. (The leader may refer to briefing notes.)

Celtic churches in the West did not lose a creation-friendly understanding.

> Augustine taught that creation was an act of God's power,
> Celtic Christians saw it as an act of God's love.
>
> *Leslie Newbiggin*

Early British churches ensured new members understood this teaching, as this ancient Celtic catechism reveals:

> What is God's will?
>> That we should live according to the laws of his creation.
>
> What is best in this world?
>> To do the will of our Maker.
>
> How do we know those laws?
>> By studying the Scriptures with devotion.
>
> What tool has our Maker provided for this study?
>> The intellect which can probe everything.
>
> And what is the fruit of study?
>> To perceive the eternal Word of God reflected in every plant and insect, every bird and animal, and every man.

Columbanus, echoing St Paul in Romans 1:20, taught church members to live with two books in their hands: the Scriptures and Creation.

How churches can be friends of the earth

In their teaching
Those who teach in the church may contact websites for information about eco-friendly congregations, spirituality and teaching resources.

In their prayer and celebration
Habitual celebration of the earth as an expression of God's life should include songs (including newly written ones) and signs of God in creation; prayers for pets and the

earth; beautifying and energising meeting places with plants, signs or paintings of creation. Each week members may bring tokens of creation and explain how these speak to them of God. The earth and animals are often blessed, sunrise, solstice and prayer walks are held.

In Jewish tradition creation is celebrated on the first day of the week, since that images the first day of creation. Churches that have daily prayer have a creation theme on Mondays, the first working day, or a creation theme on the first Sunday of each month. The Iona Community, the Community of Aidan and Hilda, and liturgists such as David Adam provide rich material to draw from.

Emerging churches, like the Jews, mark the seasons. For example, near the end of the harvest season (Feast of Tabernacles) by putting tents or shacks in gardens for a period (see Leviticus 23) and inviting relatives and neighbours in.

Discussion

In what ways are you disconnected from the earth? In what fresh ways can you mark the seasons and make a habit of celebrating God in creation?

In their earth care

1. Use energy-saving, non-polluting materials and recycled products; buy local, fair trade or organic foodstuffs; donate to ecology projects; improve the ecology of your area; build up eco-consciousness in local schools; support local ecology groups or the Agenda 21 Process initiated by the Rio Earth Summit of 1994.

2. Get out into the outdoors, cut out over-consumption and practise forgiveness.

3. Observe a day of rest on Saturday or Sunday, e.g. by being together instead of all going in different directions.

4. Make the best of any curtilage, churchyard or garden area: for wild flowers, growth of fruits or vegetables.

5. Create connections with wild places; reclaim and guard sacred spaces.

6. Create water features (early Christian churches had fountains flowing by their baptistries) and creation theme corners, thus bringing together the feminine (wells) with the masculine (square buildings).

7. Create roof gardens or peace gardens. The Bruderhof Community has a half-acre park near Nonington, Kent, which includes life-sized statues of a child, a wolf and a lamb, illustrating the prophet Isaiah's vision of peace (Isaiah 11:6-9). With other churches provide peace running tracks in the locality. (For directions call +44 (0) 1304 84 29 80.)

8. Keep allotments. One urban church provides a shed in a beautifully kept allotment for its members to keep and use. Share the produce of members, cells or households who grow their own food.

The Arusha Project is developing a Christian Country Park in Southall, London.

The town of Almolongua, Guatemala was gripped by acute poverty, violence, and witchcraft. Crop yields were low owing to arid land and poor working habits. Following the humbling and uniting of the town's church leaders, who called the people to concerted prayer, over 80 per cent became Christians. There was a social and agricultural transformation. They have planted more crops and improved the quality of the soil and the work. Now they yield large vegetables, which are sold many miles away. Radishes harvest in 40 instead of 60 days, and there are up to three harvests of some crops. The town has been nick-named America's vegetable garden. US researchers came to learn the secret. Local Christians believe it is the wisdom God gave to them as they become intimate with God. The story of this and other revived churches is told in the video Transformations.

Exercise

On a flip chart list all the suggestions made in this unit. Tick the ones you think your church could address over the next year. Now number these in order of priority.

Task group

Plan how to carry out the priority suggestions.

Hospitality – Churches as Eating and Meeting Places

Opening prayer or worship

This may include the following prayer:

You are the caller
You are the poor
You are the stranger at the door
You are the wanderer
The unfed
You are the homeless
With no bed
You are the man
Driven insane
You are the child
Crying in pain.
from David Adam, *The Edge of Glory*
(SPCK Triangle, 1985)

Bible Study

The Bible calls us to be communities of hospitality. The first household churches ate together. Read Acts 2:46.

Remember, the wider church is likened to a household. Read 1 Timothy 3:15.

Discuss

1) Church members were told that many people who had given hospitality to a stranger had welcomed an angel without realising it (Hebrews 13:2). What episode in the Old Testament does this refer to? Does any group member know of a blessing that has resulted from an act of hospitality?

2) Which stories in the four Gospels, which involve a meal, can you recall? What do these stories say to us?

Our Celtic birthright

Early community churches in Britain and Ireland outgrew houses, but they still shared meals together and with strangers. They built refectories. One or several community members were set aside for the work of hospitality. Columba's community church at Derry fed 1000 hungry people daily. Even when David's monks in Wales ate only bread themselves, they cooked appetising meals for the elderly and frail!

Changing needs

In the second millennium most churches were praying places but not eating places. In the twenty-first century church buildings that are not used for such activities as eating are ignored or vandalised. Such hospitality often resonates with people of other faiths who are better than we are at hospitality. Although in a Welfare State there is not always a physical need for churches to be eating places, there may be a social need. Sir Terence Conran, the restaurateur, predicts the emergence of the café society: 'Cafés will increasingly serve as outside offices and public spaces in which to do business.'

Examples of what some modern churches offer:

cafés,
lunch clubs,
soup kitchens,
picnic areas,
DIY refreshment facilities,
cabaret worship,
celebrations.

Members of the group may mention churches they know who provide any of these facilities.

Accommodation

In the new way of being church it will be normal for communal churches to provide accommodation in such ways as the following:

- a back packers' hostel,
- an annexe,
- units built above or beside the main church building,
- turning a redundant church building into a hermitage and retreat centre,
- establishing a local housing scheme,
- members buying houses nearby through a trust fund,
- use of space as a night shelter,
- church website giving information on B&B in members' homes.

Discuss

Which of these is most viable in your church?

An appraisal of our church – tick or leave blank

Does the church provide:

- ☐ refreshment facilities,
- ☐ refreshments after Sunday or midweek worship,
- ☐ communal meals for members,
- ☐ meals for non-members,
- ☐ a café,
- ☐ a soup kitchen,
- ☐ a picnic area,
- ☐ homes offering meals to visitors,
- ☐ other welcomers at church worship and events,
- ☐ social activities at which locals feel at home,
- ☐ overnight accommodation for visitors,
- ☐ a hostel,
- ☐ hospitality for overseas guests,
- ☐ a crèche?

No. of ticks out of fourteen: _____

Even if all or most of these things do not seem viable yet, what next step can you take?

A key to God's Kingdom

Hospitality is more even than board and lodging, it is a principle for the whole of church life. Hospitality of heart and in the way a church arranges itself is a key that unlocks God's kingdom.

A USA church describes itself as 'a community of hope proclaiming God's inclusive love, removing barriers to faith, empowering all God's people to grow in grace towards wholeness'. Its website is www.cathedral of hope.com.

You may not wish to follow that church's example, but

you may wish to pray that you will be led in an equally clear way to express hospitality in the way that is appropriate for your church at this time.

Task group

1. Plan a meal together.

2. Discuss what it would take for your church to become radically inclusive – i.e. to enable people of all ages, genders, races and abilities to enter into the heart of the congregation's life?

3. Find out about or visit churches which provide all-round hospitality.

   Some churches with cafés are The Baptist Church, Bath; King's Church, Cockermouth; The Minster, Dewsbery; St Paul's Church, Walsall; Christ Church, Woking.

4. Address the risks of hospitality, e.g. not being able to cope with the extra demands that will be made? Identify and discuss these.

5. Draw up proposals to extend your church's ability to offer rounded hospitality.

Churches as Creativity Centres

The church badly needs a face-lift,
because it is God's theatre on earth,
and he should be packing them in.
Boy George, singer

Bible Study

The first person the Bible records as being full of the Holy
Spirit is a man who is into creative arts. The first church it
records as asking people to stop donating because it has
enough is a centre of creative activity.

Listen as Exodus 35:30-35 is read aloud slowly. Then
share what strikes you.

A conclusion

We need to learn how to release the God-given creativity
in each church member, and how to make our church a
seedbed of creativity.

Discuss

What are the implications of the following statements
(4 minutes)

'My denomination is the most left-brained organisation in
the world.' *Mainline church minister*

'The agenda for the rest of your life is to make it as right-brained as it is left-brained.' *Church shaper*

Celtic inspiration

Celtic monastery churches became centres of artistic training. As they evangelised, illuminated Gospels, portable altars and inspiring plates and cups for Holy Communion were constantly being produced. The high Crosses were decorated with Bible stories. Metal work, textiles, stone or parchment were used to make artefacts. Poetry was recorded, written and illuminated. Beautiful inscriptions and epithets were carved onto pottery and jewellery. Folk heritage was recorded, ballads were composed, songs written; there was dramatic retelling of prophetic messages, storytelling, wine and mead making, and more.

The scope of church-friendly creative arts

Today these can include art, audio-visual displays, banner making, body-soul exercises, child-minding, dance, drama, flower arranging, folk crafts, gardening, high-tech presentations, iconography, landscaping, music, painting, photography, play, poetry, reading aloud, sports, storytelling, walking, websites, writing – anything that comes out of the creative flow of members.

Add to this list.

An inspiring story *(read by one person)*

Caedmon was an Anglo-Saxon farm labourer who could not read, and who had a low self-image. At a regular social gathering hosted by his monastery church at Whitby he slipped out before it was his turn to sing something. That night he dreamed that a visitor asked him to sing. 'I could not sing in front of all those people,' Caedmon told him. 'Then sing to me,' said the visitor, whose warmth melted

Caedmon. 'What should I sing about?' 'Sing about the creation of the world,' the friend replied. Glorious melody ensued as Caedmon sang his heart out. On waking, Caedmon told his supervisor of the dream, who arranged for him to talk with Bible teachers at Hilda's monastery. They taught him a Bible story and asked him to turn it into a song. Day after day Caedmon remembered a new story and put it to song. He became a lay brother in the monastery, and soon his Bible songs went the rounds of the 'Karaokes' of those days. His gift had been recognised, and he became Christianity's first pop singer in the English language.

Have two minutes' silence and share any thoughts this story evokes. One lesson is that churches need to listen to the dreams and provide 'nurseries' for the seed talents of those who relate to them.

Examples of what can be done

1. Before Presbyterian minister George McCleod's transformation, he kept 'strict controls on access to his innermost core, where the puritan carefully policed the passionate' (Ronald Ferguson's biography, published by Collins). Afterwards, through the Iona Community, theatre, art and symbol began to be restored to the church.

2. An Edinburgh church has appointed a minstrel.

3. Some churches sponsor sculptures, art and exhibition areas.

Bible Study

Read or make a resumé of Exodus chapter 36. What different skills were used in the building of that temple? (Anyone may answer.) A definition of creativity is 'Bringing something to birth'. Every person is called to bring something to birth. Spend a minute or two thinking what you like doing. How can the creative energy of it be used to bring something – anything – into being? Now share this with the group if you wish.

How to bring a congregation's creativity into flower

1. Overcome mental barriers. Teach that the Creator designed everyone to reflect God's creativity in some way. God is Beauty, as well as Truth and Goodness. People are drawn to God through the beauty of creation, the senses and the imagination. Some people seek God by turning away from these, in case these pull them away from God; and people of certain temperaments use the mind more easily than the imagination. Churches should find a place for all types, and recognise that these are in fact different forms of creativity.

   Many things stop us creating. Mrs Pavrach stopped her children from creating. She was always saying, 'You can't do that' or 'You'll never do that'. They never did. What are the Mrs Pavrachs in your life? Parents, siblings, society, fear of failure, 'it's not a proper job'? (*5 minutes*)

2. List the creative arts that are given adequate space in your church, and list creative arts you think could now be appropriately introduced.

Task group

1. In order to value and use the whole Body of Christ find out what gifts each member has, including artistic, musical, contemplative, dance, drama and poetic gifts. Plan how to affirm, develop and use these gifts.

2. Arrange for members to do the Myers-Briggs Personality Indicator tests. This helps people to release themselves and others into their natural ways of creativity. Retreats Magazine has information about some of these.

SESSION 7

A Rhythm of Prayer and Work

Introduction

Churches rooted in a corporate rhythm of prayer and work provide shade under which travellers may rest, order within which they become calm, nourishment and beauty for the soul.

> We either resonate with everything and find discord or we resonate with the deepest things of God and find rhythm.
>
> *Pastor of a London Community Church*

Moslems, who keep a rhythm of corporate prayer, borrowed this from the first-millennium Arab Christians. Fitness centres, magazines and alternative therapies recognise the importance of body-soul rhythm. Tragically, the worship of many churches is too packaged to say hello to the sun's dawning, the rain's falling, the day's dying or the season's sensing. Yet once churches become like people's monasteries it is possible to create a sense of daily rhythm, which touches and inspires a wider number and which connects them with the ebb and flow of deeper realities.

Bible Study

The Bible sets the entire story of God's saving work for humanity within the setting of a universe of rhythm. A group member reads Genesis 1:27-2:3. Pause in case someone wishes to share something that strikes them in that passage.

The Bible tells how God chooses a people and teaches them ways of reflecting that rhythm in their society, for example through one day in seven and one year in seven rest. A group member reads Exodus 20:8-11. Pause in case someone wishes to share something that strikes them in that passage.

The Bible reveals that Jews prayed in the rhythm of sunrise, midday and sunset. A group member reads Psalm 55:17. What famous Old Testament personality kept this rhythm up even in a hostile land? If no one knows, read Daniel 6:13. Really keen believers punctuated each 24-hour period seven times with prayer: Psalm 119:164.

In the New Testament Jesus models for us a rhythm of self-giving and withdrawal to a solitary place. The Saviour arranged for his most significant actions to coincide with the rhythm of the religious seasons.

Acts 2:42, 46 tell us that the early church in Jerusalem attended the prayers day by day. The first ecumenical council of the New Testament churches saw these churches as a restoration of King David's set-up, and a making good the gaps in it (Acts 15:16). This included the restoration of daily worship.

Daily prayer through the ages

In the first millennium it was normal for every large church to have daily prayers, and these were called 'People's Services'. What made them decline? Daily worship in central churches became clericalised, the form became more important than the reality. Monasteries developed long, wordy services, which suited celibate monks but which put off the general population. Celtic monastic churches felt more homely, but these were destroyed by Viking invasions. A counter-church culture developed, which encouraged prayers from pulpits or in groups, but not corporate daily prayer. However, even after the sixteenth-century Roman Catholic/Protestant divide, not only Roman Catholics, but some Anglicans and Protestant churches such as the Mennonites held daily prayer services.

Why bother now?

If this daily offering of total worship does not again become the centre of our life, our world will not be able to be transfigured or united. It will be incapable of surpassing its divisions, its imbalance, its emptiness and death, in spite of all human-centred plans to improve it.

Archimandrite George Capsanis of Mount Athos.

Discuss this apparently far-fetched statement. *(5 minutes)*

The essence of rhythm

Rhythm itself is more important than any particular form. The word rhythm comes from a Greek word (*rhuthmos*), whose root meaning is flow. Physicists are discovering that our universe has an underlying pattern; nature is full of symmetry. Every human being is a microcosm of the universe, and the Creator has built rhythm into the universe. Every human being has a circadian rhythm; our body rhythms are affected by light and dark and need them both.

Rhythm is indivisible. There is a rhythm of the seasons of the year and a rhythm of the seasons of life. Emerging churches seek to flow in these rhythms.

In emerging churches the corporate worship follows the rhythm of the natural seasons and of the church year, and observes seasons of fasting or spiritual warfare, of lamentation for the sins and hurts of society, and of joy and celebration of creation. St Thomas Church, Crookes, Sheffield has a holiday from activities during July and August, so that it has more energy for the outreach and discipling seasons that follow.

What are the ingredients of satisfying daily worship today?

Different people prefer particular ingredients, e.g.

- Scripture readings
- songs or psalms of praise
- familiar prayers
- silent reflection
- visual focus (e.g. icons, a themed prayer corner)
- fresh materials for each day or season
- music to listen to
- topical concerns
- flexible times of meeting.

Some main church streams have their own liturgies. Others, within as well as outside these denominations, use simpler, more flexible patterns, perhaps from contemporary communities or from David Adam's *The Rhythm of Life*. Other churches, whether or not they use these liturgies, adopt a simple structure such as praise, self-offering, Bible reading, silent reflection, prayers for others. They may combine this with a breakfast or supper on one or more days. Churches that meet just once a day vary greatly in the times when they meet, from early morning to mid-morning to early evening to before bedtime.

Some adopt a theme for each day, and transfer these to cards or CDs, which every member can use wherever they are:

Monday:	Creation and the world of work
Tuesday:	Incarnation, reconciliation, justice and peace
Wednesday:	Healing and education
Thursday:	Unity, community, sacrament and creative arts
Friday:	The Cross and the world's broken people (fast day)
Saturday:	Sports and saints
Sunday:	Resurrection and renewal of church and society

There is a weekly rhythm of daily prayer together, a common meal on Thursday, fasting and prayer round the Cross on Friday and regular blessings in homes. Each local church should have ingredients that are unique to itself. Some, for example, pray for people in a particular street on a daily rota basis. Others pick out names from a box containing prayer request slips.

Exercises

Make a list of the ingredients most members of your group think should be in daily services.

- Is there something distinctive to your situation, which you would regularly include?

- What times of day are the best for your church to have prayer together? (They might vary from day to day.)

- Share ideas for creating visual focal points, or themed prayer corners.

- Does/how can your church programme reflect the rhythm of the Christian and natural seasons?

- Does/how can your church reflect the rhythm of the week?
- Does/how can your church reflect the rhythm of the day?
- Does/how can your church provide rest periods and retreats?
- Does/how can the church sponsor work projects?
- Does/how can your church support its members in their work place?
- Does/how can your church support the work centres in its area?
- Does/how can your church keep Sunday special?

Task group

Invite feedback from the church and pilot a planned pattern of daily prayer.

Turning Church Buildings
into Spiritual Homes

*(This session is only suitable for churches who own
or manage their own property)*

Few church buildings in Britain have the feel and function of a spiritual home; secularising drives have marginalised them. Yet the 24-hour society has arrived. Church buildings that are closed most of this time are a turn-off. They get vandalised. People do not vandalise buildings which they feel are there for them. Researchers find that the public wants shops, etc. to be more like homes; hence shops are bringing 'body and soul' facilities under one roof, from cafés to advice centres.

Define a spiritual home

'A place where people of different temperaments and ages can relax amid familiar objects, pray, meet and eat in a relaxing atmosphere, celebrate the important things in life, blow their top, find spaces for privacy, silence, beauty or study.' How would you define it?

Bible Study

- Read 1 Timothy 3:15. The New Testament often describes the church as a home or household.

- Read Matthew 21:13. Churches should be places where people of all backgrounds and races may be drawn to pray without being got at.

- Read John 14:2. It should mirror Jesus' teaching about our heavenly home – a place with many rooms, that is, something to suit every temperament.

- After a pause share anything that struck you in these Scripture verses.

Celtic churches

Celtic churches were homely centres of community, which combined devotional, social, work and study activities.

Features of church buildings that are spiritual homes

Warm and accessible
How can easy chairs, toilets, car parking, notice boards, loop systems, sign language, wheelchair access, carpets, heating best create this?

An eating place as well as a praying place
What refreshment facilities and eating occasions can be established?

A work and creative place
Vacuum cleaner inventor James Dyson predicts that new technology heralds the return of the artisan, the gifted creator of desirable goods. Creative artists and artisans will soon have the means to use church premises even in rural areas. What services and activities can bless the interests, work, sport and life of the neighbourhood?

A lived-in, or at least a safe place – physically and emotionally
Can accommodation be built into or near the church building? Can a rota of staff employ their time in pursuits such as cleaning, typing, sewing, studio recording, crafts or study? Can the church office be sited there? Can children and parents be made to feel accepted and relaxed by provision of a playroom, nappy changing room or crèche room?

Conducive to different styles of spirituality
Different styles of prayer should be expressed in the one building, so that people of different temperaments feel relaxed. Some churches have removed fixed pews to create spaces for dance, displays, prayer postures, candles, icons, fountains and creation foci.

A healing and humane place
How can joys, sorrows, anger, questioning, celebrations, anniversaries, ceilidhs, memorial gatherings be encouraged?

Educational and ecumenical
Are there learning resources, courses, videos, books, a 'church trail', digital interpretations of the church's story, items familiar to members of other church streams?

A centre for spiritual development, meditation and soul friendship

See the photocopiable questionnaire on the following pages

The Diamond Award for your church building

Imagine you are an objective and shrewd Inspector representing those who are not drawn to your church building. Award your main church building diamond ratings on a scale of 0 to 5 using the following checklist (put a figure in the square):

☐ Heated and open on weekdays

☐ Wide, welcoming entrance way

☐ Visitors' Book

☐ Free car parking or easy public transport

☐ Prayer Requests Board

☐ No off-putting churchy publicity or paraphernalia

☐ Toilets

☐ Kitchen

☐ Telephone and office

☐ Shop

☐ Spaces where it's OK to stay undisturbed in quiet

☐ Café

☐ Has a warm, lived-in, emotional feel

☐ Carpets and easy chairs

☐ Refreshment facilities through the week

☐ Children's play and display area

☐ Nappy changing room

☐ Crèche

☐ Space for movement, dance etc

☐ Places and computers for private study

☐ Book, DVD and resources library

☐ Creation of themed corner in building or garden, or a
well or fountain

☐ Services and symbols of healing

☐ Book of Remembrance (added to by bereaved people)

☐ Graveyard or Garden of Remembrance in use

☐ Exhibition areas for art, poetry, photography

☐ Hosts school visits

☐ Educationally effective church trail leaflet or guide

☐ Advice facility, e.g. local information, helping
agencies, guidance on wills

☐ Educational resources in the building
(e.g. videos of what goes on in the church)

☐ Computers/website/cyber café

☐ Hosts celebrations of significance to a cross-section of
the neighbourhood groups (give examples)

☐ Hosts celebrations of significance to a cross-section of
families (e.g. anniversaries)

☐ Includes song books, symbols, etc. of other church streams

☐ Includes items that connect with ethnic or other local
minorities

☐ Easy access and facilities for the handicapped

Add up your total number of diamonds. The maximum you could get is 150. Now identify five priorities you could introduce.

During the prayer time, or later, circle the building (physically or in your imagination) and pray for it and for the people for whom it could become a spiritual home.

Task group

Visit some church buildings that have become multi-resource centres:

- St Mark's, Beckton, London has a gym
- Christ Church Community Project, Kingsmead Estate, nr Hackney Marsh
- Christ Church, Woking
- Dewsbery Minster Church
- St Paul's in the Crossing, Walsall
- Kingsway Centre, Liverpool
- Holy Trinity, Hounslow

SESSION 9

Weaving the Strands Together

During the second millennium the great strands of Christ's universal church became separated. These strands include:

Catholic –   the focus is community around
             Holy Communion

Protestant –   the focus is personal conversion around
               the Bible

Orthodox –   the focus is the living tradition of prayer
             in the liturgy and in the heart

There are other strands, e.g. Pentecostal, where the focus is the experience of the person and gifts of the Holy Spirit.

Name any other strand that is important to you.

Bible Study

The Bible teaches that there is only one church. It likens this to a human body. Christ is like the head of the body. Each local congregation or group is like a limb or an eye.

Read aloud Ephesians 4:4-6, 15-16; 5:29. Reflect on these verses in silence. *(5 minutes)*

Share anything in them that strikes you as important enough to require a response. *(7 minutes)*

Now let's jump from the original church to the separated strands of today's church. Many leaders and members of these strands sincerely believe that the one true Church of which the Bible speaks is comprised of their strand, and that the way to unity is to convince separated brothers and sisters to return to the fold (their strand).

But what if the fullness of Christ's Body can only be attained if each strand is like a limb that recognises that it does not contain in itself the fullness of Christ's Body? For example, one church strand despises other strands – and thereby ceases to reflect Christ's humble love to the world. Another church proselytises other Christians without a basis of trust – and thereby ceases to reflect Christ's solidarity with others.

Read 1 Corinthians 12:14-20. The fragmentation of Christianity is a sin, and a cause of stumbling to believers and seekers, many of whom now refuse to be defined by a protest movement of 450 years ago (the Catholic/Protestant divide known as the Reformation) or by the divide between the Eastern Orthodox and Western Churches of 1054.

In the early church in Celtic lands these strands were not separated. The church was catholic – part of the one universal church – sharing the same Scriptures, creeds and forms of ministry. It looked to the focal points of unity going back to the apostles – Peter in Rome, John in Ephesus. It was Bible-based, and it was Spirit-led.

Is God calling us to re-unite these strands in the third millennium? Unity schemes from the top down have made some progress, but not breakthrough.

We need to weave the strands together at the grass roots. This is not just patching together, however. In the Celtic model we understand that God is still 'weaving the cloth'.

To put it another way, the Acts of the Apostles is not just a finished book in the Bible, it is still being written.

In this model, we long that all shall be immersed daily in the precious Triune God – this can be seen as the fulfilment of the ideals of Baptists.

We see Christ in the face of the stranger or foe as well as in the neighbour – this echoes the Quaker insight that 'there is that of God in each person'.

Here are three ways of weaving:

1. A group exercise to get inside the mind of another strand
The group members stand in a line. Each lays a hand on the head of the next person. The first person represents Jesus ordaining an apostle, the second person represents an apostle ordaining a bishop, and so on. This idea is called apostolic succession and is thought to be Jesus' way of ensuring that his ministry continues.

Now the group members again stand in a line but this time each represents any member of the church. They pass a Bible down from the first to the last. This idea is the priesthood of all believers, who, it is thought, can know Jesus directly through the Bible.

Now the group members form a circle, and hold out their arms to invite the Holy Spirit to inwardly reveal to them who should follow the different callings, such as apostle, prophet, pastor, healer, teacher.

When you have completed this exercise share what you sensed might be of God in these three ways of being church.

2. Make your own a spiritual treasure from each strand

This cannot be simulated. It may take the rest of your life.

One person might, for example, learn to contemplate in the way of the Catholic Spanish mystics such as John of the Cross; embrace the Puritan tradition of William Law or John Bunyan; and pray the Jesus Prayer in the spirit of Seraphim of Russia. Name classic spiritualities from different strands that you know of or would like to explore.

3. Practise accepting yourself as a pilgrim whose companions you do not choose

When we come to accept our vulnerability we become connected with others who are vulnerable. A fellowship of the 'poor in spirit' spans the denominations and the centuries.

Task group

1. Instead of adding yet another layer of activity to your church, think out how to deepen trust between your church and others from different strands.

2. Propose ways of incorporating insights from different strands in your worship, programme and teaching.

SESSION 10

People-friendly Mission

The fifth- to seventh-century Celtic mission was unusually effective in winning Irish, British and English pagan populations to God. The top-down, packaged Roman model of mission was less effective. This model was reflected in second-millennium church styles of mission, which we inherit and which are losing their effectiveness.

Bible Study

Jesus reached out to people, loved them as they were, stood in their shoes and laid down his life for them. He was able to become one with the people in all things except sin because he remained one with his divine Father at all times. Because he was secure, he did not pressurise others. He was able within himself to lose earthly power, and so became king of hearts.

His critics, the Pharisees, had big evangelistic campaigns and would traverse the earth to gain one convert, but failed to turn round the hearts of the people. Why? They imposed their culture on the people, whereas Jesus made himself one with them.

Read Matthew 23:13-15; Mark 9:40 and 1 Corinthians 9:19-23. After 2 minutes' silent reflection share what thoughts came to you as to how you can 'become like' an unchurched section of society.

The Irish way of mission

In 'Celtic' Christianity true evangelism begins within the culture and flows out of love for the whole person. It grows out of relationships. It gives God and people time and space. It is natural.

In Celtic mission there are three elements:

- good news to share,

- a model of what this means (churches that help the needy, motivate seekers and offer ceaseless prayer),

- a fellow feeling for others that enables the Christian to get inside their skin.

Without all three elements mission often fails.

Saint Patrick won much of fifth-century pagan Ireland to Christ. He shared his vulnerability with the people. He began his mission by accepting an invitation from a good pagan to stay in his home. He discerned certain gospel-friendly 'handles', which he could turn to God's advantage, such as prophecies by Druids that a new religion would come to their land. He caught the attention of everyone by holding a big bonfire to celebrate Christ's resurrection. He spent time with God discerning who were the naturally good people who would welcome a good person when they met one. He took prime time to befriend the natural leaders (people who could open doors) and their extended families.

Group meditation: Befriending unchurched people of goodwill

Take time to become aware of the people in an area of your life. Hold them before God. Which ones stand out as being open to goodness? Visualise spending time with the person who seems most open and accessible, giving them opportunity to share what is important to them, what they long for, and giving time to share what is important to you. *(5 minutes' silence; 5 minutes' sharing)*

Discussion

A Muslim congregation has adapted Christian hymns such as 'Abide with me' for use at funerals. What might be an adaptation for a Christian Church, in a Muslim area?

A culture-friendly Church mission statement

Read aloud this mission statement of one church:

> Our policy is to offer unconditional love for Christ's sake to every person within this parish and to every person who is drawn to us. We will maintain nothing that unnecessarily causes their faith to stumble – anachronistic ways, words that alienate or confuse. We will do nothing that makes them feel excluded or inferior. We will aim to be present at their point of need, as far as God gives us resources.
>
> We say to them:
> We will bless your babies and homes.
> The church building is open every day.
> We invite you to share food and silence.

Note points to include from this in a mission statement for your church.

Justice

Everyone who struggles for justice is working for God's reign. The emerging Church values everything that is in tune with its struggle to set up God's reign. A church that tries only to keep itself pure and uncontaminated would not be a church of God's service to people.

Emerging churches tithe their income to give to the needy, build bridges between hostile groups, and speak out for the poor and unjustly treated.

Modern examples of culture-friendly mission

Churches got together in an area of Liverpool and invited people in the shops and streets to a barbecue, free, at the Podium. Two bands were on the shopping streets during the days preceding this, giving out invitations. 6600 were fed. 'At last the church is doing what it should always have been doing,' said a guest.

In another area Churches Together took a daffodil to each patient in the local hospital at Easter.

Choose one or more of the following issues to discuss:

1. What Gospel-friendly trends do we discern in our society?

2. Celtic Christians met at the people's natural gathering places
Some significant gathering places today are cafés, pubs, parks, leisure centres, schools, shopping centres, health centres and airports.
What gathering places are significant for people today in your area? How can you develop a Christian presence in one of these?

3. Only a minority now follow mainstream religion
However, the Alister Hardy Research Unit has discovered that nearly two thirds of the British population admit to having religious experiences.
Mike Pilavachi, who has started the Soul Survivor

church near Watford, likens the traditional Anglican church, which he says he loves, to a high class French restaurant whose cuisine and menu is entirely French. He likens churches such as Soul Survivor to McDonald's – cheap, cheerful and accessible – where most of the population feel more at home. Assuming that most unchurched children and adults have spirituality, and that more British people are at home in McDonalds than in a French restaurant, what signs of unchurched people's spirituality have you noticed? What meeting place would they find most natural? What would make it easy to meet them there?

Christian presence outside the hubs

1. Give examples of Churches you know which have places of Christian presence other than their main building.

2. Tick which of the following Christian presences exist in the area your church relates to:

- *poustinias* or prayer huts that anyone can apply to use
- Christian café or shop
- counselling, advice or listening agency
- Christian pub, guesthouse
- Christian school
- Christian organisations in non-church buildings, chaplaincies in schools, homes, etc.
- study courses
- meditation
- alternative or family worship
- house groups
- routine pastoral visits
- music or singing events
- body-soul exercise classes
- alternative healing service
- cyber café or web link up

3. Add to this list of Christian presences those that exist outside the area served by your church.

Task group

Map the area for which you have concern. Locate the Christian presences on it (including the activities of any Christian church). Note the gaps. Decide which Christian services you can take to the people rather than requiring them to come to the existing church. Put the most achievable of these in order of priority and plan how to develop them.

Draw up a mission statement agreed by the church.

Turning Congregations into Communities

This course has explored some key features of emerging churches. The most important feature has been left until now. Unless a congregation becomes a community that serves others it will not be possible to sustain these other features.

But to turn a Sunday-only collection of churchgoers into a community is a humanly impossible task. By a community we mean a seven-days-a-week congregation which prays and works together.

Only certain churches are fitted to attempt this task. Therefore the first step is to discern where our church lies on a spectrum. When we know that, we can discern whether our church has the potential to become a community, or what more limited tasks it can undertake.

Churches that can't be a multi-faceted community

Most small and many middle-sized churches cannot provide the spectrum of features that people expect of a church, nor the will to finance traditional church structures. (Occasionally, however, a community church can grow out of a small group that shares, e.g. a house.)

If the group that sustains such a 'church' is freed from expectations of 'keeping up church' it can become an effective resource group for a particular purpose. Here are some examples of what former churches, which have become resource groups, can provide:

- a monthly all-age service in a school
- a monthly alternative service in a pub
- a monthly traditional service in sheltered housing
- a parents' and toddlers' club
- a household fellowship or cell church.

Add to this list.

It requires clear thinking, courage and humility to make this change. In denominations it may mean refusing to collude with their inappropriate structures.

Discuss

Tick the categories that best describe your church.

- ☐ Enough energies and resources to evolve into a community hub church
- ☐ Is stuck with decline, and there is no point in trying to change this
- ☐ Would benefit by ceasing to be 'a church' and becoming a resource group

If your church is not in the first category you can choose either to omit the following material and use the time to talk and pray about how you can best bring your present situation to a close and develop as a resource group, or to continue the course in order to become more aware of possibilities in the wider church. A former church that becomes a resource agency needs a hub church to which it can relate. This also applies if your church is in the first category but you are not involved in its leadership.

Celtic community churches

Although it is difficult to turn a congregation into a community, it has been done before. From the sixth century the churches were communities, which were the hub of their society's life.

Steps in turning a congregation into a community

Step 1: Lay down your life for the place or community to which God calls you

The Revd Graham Pulkingham, when called to the inner city parish in Houston, USA, wrote: 'I became so identified with the neighbourhood as to be baptised in its bondage and pain.' This requires unconditional commitment from leaders, not temporary contracts. This can be on a small scale, for example, two or three people based in a home.

Questions

1. Am I in the place of God's calling? Consider this on your own later.

2. What does if mean for me to lay down my life for this place? Discuss if you wish.

Step 2: Form a core servant community of daily prayer

The core group should, of course, be authorised by the appropriate church authorities. It should pray together daily and incarnate steps four to seven. Some might move to a home near the church building; others might share salaries to free others for voluntary work. Discuss examples or possibilities of salary or work sharing.

Step 3: Find and share a vision

Wait on God for a vision. Through due process, when this is owned by the church, it should be put on a logo, so it can be read at a glance (Habakkuk 2:2).

Step 4: Covenant to keep core values

The core community that interacts through the week needs to covenant to live by some agreed core values, or a Rule of Life, which includes ways of building up one another and society (as in Session 9).

Step 5: Turn the church building into a spiritual home

Finally, once the praying community is alive and well, the church building needs to be turned into a multi-purpose resource centre that is also a spiritual home (as in Session 8).

Bible Study

Read Acts 2:42-47

What did those early church members do daily? What did those in paid employment do? What lessons can we learn from this?

Exercise

1. Tick or leave blank

☐ Does your congregation have daily public prayer? If not, what next step could it take to provide worship more than one day a week?

☐ Is there a group of people (besides the minister's) who service the prayer or work at the church building during the week?

☐ Has this group been publicly commissioned or affirmed by the congregation's leadership?

☐ Is this group (core community) bound together by a shared statement of values, or Rule of Life?

☐ Is this core community recognised and released by local and/or wider church authorities (e.g. deacons, diocese, circuit) so that there are not conflicting lines of accountability?

☐ If there is no such core group, how do you assess the potential for developing this?

☐ Today some congregations seek to restore the household church, e.g. through cells, or through household celebrations such as a Friday Shabat meal. Does your congregation have cells? Home groups? Regular household celebrations that are common to more than one household?

2. Where the answer is 'no', decide what you can do about this.

Draw up a pattern for your church of 1) daily corporate prayer, 2) regular hospitality, 3) discipling of others, and 4) seasonal outreach, allocating members of the group to one of these.

Task group
Bring a community hub church into being by using the insights gleaned from this course.

Cells, Households
and Villages of God

*(Note: This final session is about the spirit and skills of
leadership, and applies to any who help to lead in any
sector of their church.)*

If the course group does not include leaders or potential
leaders you may choose either to end the course now, or to
use the final session to share ways in which God has spoken
to you through the course and to plan and pray for the
future. If possible this should be in the setting of a household
shared meal, however simple, and a house blessing. Create
a good ambience, e.g. with the use of music, flowers or
candles. After the first course, proceed with the course
material below. After any dessert, bless the house you are
eating in. Follow this by worship, if desired, and pray a
blessing on the homes of each person present.

An example of a household meal is included in *The Celtic
Prayer Book,* Volume Three, *Healing the Land: natural seasons,
sacraments and special services* (Kevin Mayhew).

Introduction

A snapshot view of Britain's churches looks like a pole. Cells and household groups at one end of the pole and hub churches at the other end look set to sprout, but many congregations in the middle look set to die unless they can be broken off and rerooted.

Cells and households

Cell churches are growing across the world. These take several forms. In some forms, a cross-section of Christians commit to meet weekly for 'the 4 Ws': welcome, worship, word, witness. The cell is responsible for pastoral care and witness. In some cases the cell's priorities override those of a larger Sunday congregation which sponsored them, in other cases they serve the congregation. In many cases the cell commits to pray for non-Christian friends of members and welcome them to their meetings. Thus the cell commits to subdivide when it reaches a maximum number.

The benefits of cells are obvious. They can meet the need for real, intimate relationships and disciplings, which a larger congregation cannot provide.

Since ample literature on cell church is available, this course does not explore cells further. The website of Cell UK (part of Youth With a Mission) is www.cellchurch.co.uk

The 'Celtic' understanding of church embraces many cell church principles but it stresses two further dimensions:

1. Cells are not sufficient to themselves.
2. Organic patterns are better than contrived ones.

Cells need to relate to a hub because:

- A finger fulfils its purpose only if it's connected to the body.
- Cell leaders are often overwhelmed by the stress involved in such responsibility.

- Some types (e.g. contemplatives) thrive better outside cells.
- Some Christians are called to resource hubs rather than to be confined to cells.
- Both Christians and the general public need a hub to refer to.

Those churches that conclude that cells are not for them, or are too pressurised, may consider the household church an option.

Households

Often loyal church helpers get run down, like a machine. Their work and society create overload, and church, instead of redeeming this, imposes yet more overload. Some cease to attend an organised church, others become frustrated church 'props'. Is there a third way?

In the Jewish and Celtic traditions the household becomes a main expression of 'church'. Members can follow natural patterns of praise and reflective sharing, which do not involve committees, rehearsals, etc.

St Patrick's Church, Hove, blesses the home of each church member every year. Households meet for a weekly or monthly meal when each person is present to the other and listens to their journey since the last household meal. The Bible or the life of a saint may be reflected upon. There may be silence and singing.

Households develop prayers and rituals for significant daily and occasional happenings.

This is more natural, and organic, than cells and can achieve similar aims. It may become an extended spiritual family or may invite a different guest whenever it meets.

A household's links with a Sunday congregation are continued, for example, through participation in worship, events and networking.

Hub churches

Many mobile Christians, cells, and small churches cannot flourish unless there are centres of stability, prayer, resource and hospitality to which they can relate. A hub church is a:

- prayer centre serviced by some whose main calling is prayer
- multi-resource centre – serviced by some whose main calling is hospitality and others whose main calling is discipling existing or new church members
- covenanted, organic, relational community
- resource for mission groups, cells, church plants which relate to it.

In the Church of England there are calls for the return of the minster model. But this is a coming together of clergy. It is still top-down, not growing out of the natural people patterns.

An alternative is the Celtic monastery model. This refers to faith communities where there is a coming together of people who are vulnerable and open to God, whether they are from the top or the bottom of the social pile, ordained or in other jobs, married or single. Many different activities go on each day as people come and go, and at its heart is a core of people upholding a rhythm of prayer. Warehouse churches are a modern echo of this.

Exercise – creating a momentary monastery

In the following exercise each person places themselves in one of three circles, not according to what they presently do, or what their conditioning tells them they ought to do, but according to their deepest innate desire. The three circles are represented by hearts, hands and legs. Those whose dominant desire is to use their hearts, to be available daily for prayer, rather like Mary who sat at the feet of Jesus (Luke 10:38-42), kneel in the centre. Those whose dominant desire is to serve others through the ministries of Christ's Church (from pastoral care to making cups of tea) stand around the kneeling group, with their hands lifted to God. Those whose main calling is to serve God in the world outside the monastery, though valuing the support and the link with the monastery, walk in a circle around the people with their hands raised.

Circle 1 – hearts and heads
Circle 2 – hands
Circle 3 – feet

Divide the 'hearts', the 'hands', and the 'feet' into three groups. Invite the 'heart' members to suggest ways in which they can become more available at the church's main place of meeting – to be, to pray, to listen. Invite the 'hands' members to suggest ways they can be set free to serve in harmony with the hearts and the other hands. Invite the 'feet' to suggest ways they can regularly, even if infrequently, relate to the hub. Come together to share conclusions.

Task group

1. Does your congregation have cells? Home groups? Regular household celebrations that are common to more than one household? Where the answer is 'no', decide what you can do about this.

2. Arrange a person-to-person appraisal with each willing member of the congregation who has regular duties. Find out which duties are preventing them from 'just hanging out with God' in their homes.

3. Make contact with embryo warehouse churches or villages of God. Identify lessons your church can learn and proposals you can implement.

4. In the light of your findings, make proposals for simplifying church activities or reshuffling those responsible for them.

Follow-up

We would like to hear from you. E-mail your responses, or examples of changing churches, to the Community of Aidan and Hilda, website www.aidan.org.uk. These will be included in its 'Models for the Emerging Church' pages. Website manager's e-mail: s.dale@ntlworld.com.

OPTIONAL EXTRAS

A. Values

Ninety-five per cent of the church is about producing. It can't conceive of a lifestyle based on spaces for solitude and hospitality.

a church leader

When we are not surrounded by family – and nature – we (and churches) make decisions in a fragmented way.

a church leader

Bible Study

Jesus called people to live by a set of values, which have become known as the Beatitudes, or Beautiful Attitudes. Read Matthew 5:1-12. If churches had taken the Beatitudes as seriously as the Creeds, what would be different? *(5 minutes' silent visualisation; 5 minutes' sharing)*

Celtic churches

Each Celtic church did live by a set of gospel values, which they called a Rule. The core (married and celibate, lay and ordained) committed to the Rule. Others met with a soul friend from this core, and adopted elements of the Rule for their own lives.

The following are paraphrased items from a Rule Columbanus drew up. Each item can be read by one or more, followed by a pause:

- Let our bearing towards one another be that of Christ, honouring and listening intently to one another.
- Never grumble or hit back, or judge another.
- Only speak when God gives you something to say.
- Avoid mindless or boastful talk.
- Eat and drink nothing that overloads the stomach or confuses the mind.
- Possess only what you need or can offer as love gifts.
- Live simply in order to purge vices and foster perpetual love of God.
- Cultivate humility and purity.
- Follow the rhythm of the seasons in prayer.
- Pay heed to the season of your life, to your temperament, ability, and energy levels.
- The ceaseless prayer of the heart, not external uniformity, is what binds everyone together.
- Develop wisdom, balance, wholeness, the fruits of the Spirit, discernment of good and evil and of what justice requires.

Have five minutes' silence during which anyone may write down any item they feel is important for their church to adopt. Share these.

Building up a church-values statement

Some churches draw up a statement of values as well as a mission statement. This is sometimes called a covenant.

Before engaging in this process it is wise to learn from other faith communities. For example, from L'Arche communities we may learn about forgiveness, providing emotional space and quality of listening, which respects everything that is most beautiful and true in the other.

One minister occasionally reads this extract from the Rule of the Taizé Community at church meetings: 'Express in a few words what you feel conforms most closely to God's plan, without imagining that you can impose it.'

The Anamchara Community Church, Adelaide, has woven together the values of the Vineyard Church with those of the Community of Aidan and Hilda. After each section is read by a reader, briefly discuss and list any items you think your church should adopt.

Pursuit of God

The Community Church is a body of Christians who, before all else, are wholly available to the Holy Trinity and wholeheartedly committed to the way of Jesus as revealed to us in the Bible. The Bible is at the heart of our study.

Discipleship

As disciples of Jesus we are committed to ongoing learning, therefore we commit ourselves to study the Scriptures, the great teachers and saints of the church, and to learn from the experience of the Holy Spirit at work in God's people.

Journey

We see ourselves as 'a church without walls', a community called to live by faith. Therefore we regularly wait on God to show us what we should let go and what we should make our priorities. We encourage members and the church to discern these things with the help of a soul friend.

Rhythm

We seek to follow a rhythm of prayer, witness, study, work, hospitality and leisure which safeguards spaces that enable us to be fully human.

Spiritual Initiative

We wish to be alert, through constant intercession and reflection, to those things that undermine God's kingdom in our part of the earth being as it is in heaven, and we wish to take initiative for good.

Simplicity and generosity

We seek to be simple and natural in our lifestyle, and to give away what is surplus to our needs, not drawing attention to ourselves.

Earth care

We seek to have a loving relationship with the whole of creation, seeing it as an expression of God, and exercising self-restraint in our use of created things. In our worship we will reflect the seasons and celebrate God's presence in creation.

Wholeness

In a society and church which is fragmented and selfishly individualistic, we seek to relate sensitively to the web of life, to the web of human community, and to seek the healing of the land. We seek healing and a balance of mind and body.

Openness and risk

We are willing to be vulnerable, to listen deeply to God in the Scriptures, in the cries of the people, in prophecy and in ourselves as we sift what is heard. We expect members to learn through trial and error and are patient with their weaknesses while they learn.

Unity

We commit ourselves to be in solidarity with the human race, and with the worldwide Body of Christ on earth and in heaven. We will be humble and loving towards all fellow Christians, and be attentive to those in oversight of other churches. We seek to weave together the strands of Christianity which have become separated such as the biblical, the catholic and the charismatic, for we believe that the church is never one or the other, but always all three.

Mission and mercy
We stand with the poor and against injustice. We offer hospitality to those in true need, and take trouble to share our faith with those who lack it. Care for people is our highest priority after submission to God. We seek to integrate biblical truth into everyday life, and so impact our society.

An emerging church is likely to include such core values as these:

1. Integrity (cf. 2 Corinthians 4:1-2)
Share weaknesses and fears; live in the light.

2. Respect
Aidan did not fear to speak out on behalf of the marginalised when he was with the wealthy or powerful.

3. Love
The Rule of Columba, which Aidan and Hilda would have adopted, may have included 'Forgiveness from the heart for everyone', which is part of a Rule from the following century which is attributed to Columba.

4. Welcome
Because the core were committed to the Rule, every neighbour could belong and feel welcome without their unredeemed values taking over the church. 'He who is not against me is for me.'

Discuss
What do you think might be God's distinctive call for your church?

Exercise

A person appointed by the leader brings together the above core values and others that the group believes should be put forward for consideration by the church. This is later given to the church leadership.

Task group

Using this list as a basis, engage the whole church in a similar process and produce an agreed values statement.

A statement is useless if it is not lived. Appraise church meetings in the light of these values and seek to motivate church members to live by them.

OPTIONAL EXTRAS

B. Inspired leadership

Good leaders grow people, bad leaders stunt them.
Good leaders serve their followers, bad leaders
enslave them.
Sir Adrian Cadbury, former head of Cadbury Schweppes

Some quotes about uninspired church leaders

(tick any that ring a bell)

- Jack or Jill of all trades.
- They hide behind desks.
- They cling to their own establishment.
- They live on overdrive.
- The spiritual depth born of stillness evades them.
- Pastors confuse loving people with meeting their expectations.
- Leaders who are not secure in their own identity in God become hostage to what is not of God in their people.
- Stipendiary clergy who try to follow the flow of God in the hearts of their people feel strangled by the machine; overseers, who should be fathers to their flocks sink under mountains of paper.

What factors dispirit church leaders?

(tick any that ring a bell; add others)

- A congregation whose mindset is to preserve the past rather than reach out to the unchurched.
- The post-modern supermarket habits of our regular members, who come to church when it suits them, but expect the minister to be always there for them.
- The bureaucratic Diocesan/other system.
- Colleagues who are too threatened or busy to listen.
- Distant bishops/overseers.

Advice to leaders from people 'out there'

'Visit factories, nursing homes, schools.' 'Go talk to the Job Centre.' 'Read *The Sun.*'

What are people looking for? 'Basically for spiritual wisdom to deal with the pressures and relationships of day to day life.' (Researched by Mark Green, Vice-Principal of London Bible College, in *Anvil*, Vol. 14, No. 4, 1997)

'I am looking for leadership which is earthy, masculine, real, motherly and has a deep love which is reliable. An awful lot of godliness is up in the air. If you lean on it, it falls flat. Power corrupts. Absolute power corrupts absolutely.'

Bible Study

Read Exodus 18:17-27

This passage illustrates four principles of good leadership:

Be governed by God's calling, not career (verse 19).

Reproduce God's life and callings in others (verse 20).

Learn to build teams and to delegate (verse 25).

Be holistic – don't artificially separate family and work (v 24).

What else do you learn from this passage?

Learning from leaders in other walks of life

A shift is beginning from the maintenance of an unviable system to discipling those who ask to be discipled. In order to do this the leader needs clarity to identify priorities, courage to say 'no' to things that are secondary, skill to manage change and love.

The American psychologist Daniel Goleman, in his groundbreaking book *Emotional Intelligence*, concludes that emotional rather than rational intelligence marks out the true leader. Leadership skills researcher Des Dearlove suggests someone who failed school exams, like Richard Branson, can make a better leader than an Oxbridge don because his 'emotional intelligence' is more keenly developed.

Former Olympic yachtsman Tony Morgan, now Director of The Industrial Society, says 'liberating leaders' establish trust and good flow between fellow leaders, managers and employees; they 'create a culture where people realise it is OK to own up to a mistake or breakdown and to learn from them.'

The Industrial Society's Survey, *Liberating Leadership 1999*, identifies the five weakest areas of leadership as insensitivity to people's feelings, failure to recognise others' stress, failure to develop and guide staff, failure to encourage feedback on their own performance, and failure to consult before making decisions. The leaders in the top half of the rating show more humility and awareness of their own shortcomings.

Exercise

Recall one time when you failed. Share this if you wish.

Celtic style leadership traits

The leaders of the early Celtic Christian communities were the natural leaders of that people. They were spiritual fathers or mothers whose leadership styles reflected their personality, honed in sacrificial love. They worked with a soul friend to strip away what is false, and thus learned to be themselves. They developed discernment of spirits. If a leader is not true to themselves, they are modelling falsity to their members.

Some principles of church leadership

1. Pray until you discern God's priorities. Discard, delegate, or minimise all jobs that do not further these priorities.

2. Disciple the spiritual family. If your church is small, you disciple it as Jesus discipled the 12 apostles. If it is large, you disciple the leaders and pastors who will disciple the members. Make sure that the strongest are stretched and the weakest are guarded.

3. Allow yourself to be vulnerable. 'Never trust a leader who walks without a limp' (John Wimber).

4. Have the courage to act. The true servant leader is strong, not weak. Leaders in the retreating church postponed the painful decisions that were necessary to turn things round, for fear of the short-term pain and controversy. Emerging church leaders grasp the nettle first of all, and then enjoy the fruits.

5. Acquire the skills you need to realise these priorities.

6. Be accountable. All church leaders are prone to confuse their own ego with the will of God, and to impose the agenda of their own ego in the guise of religion. In the Celtic Church, leadership was often given to those who renounced personal property and who were accountable to another.

7. Love your people for who they are, not for what they do. A new minister brought his exciting agenda to its members; they intuited that he did not love them for themselves, but only if they were fodder for his plans. The minister realised this. He decided that, instead of laying 'his stuff' on to his congregation, he would love them for themselves, and help to draw out what was of God in 'their stuff'. It was not long before the members realised that this was 'a new deal', and started to love him. That congregation is now a community.

The final worship is an opportunity for members to rededicate themselves to God and to pray for one another to be filled and equipped by the Holy Spirit.

Task group

Invite a suitable person to be a soul friend or consultant to your leadership group and to appraise and facilitate it in the light of these principles.

Appendices

1. Examples of churches that are 'breaking the mould'
2. A spiritual audit of a neighbourhood
3. The church as a stool with three legs (diagram)
4. Networking the neighbourhood – a process for neighbourhood church
5. Recommended further reading

APPENDIX 1

Examples of churches that are 'breaking the mould'

St Thomas Church, Crookes, Sheffield, is a hub church, linked to some thirty smaller churches, which is developing a monastic missionary order.

The Soul Survivor Church, Watford, heads up the Soul Survivor youth movement.

The Warham Community is a resource and worship network linking up those who have completed Alpha courses across villages in Berkshire and Hampshire.

St Mary's, Thame, is a missionary family of congregations.

Information about Anglican network (i.e. non-parochial) churches may be obtained from Anglican Church Planting Initiatives at www.acpi.org.uk

Orbiston Parish Church, Lanarkshire, provides breakfasts, a food co-operative, and workshops.*

The United Reformed Church in Bromley-by-Bow houses a health centre.

Antioch Church, Llanelli, has elements of 'God's village' as described in Chapter 7.

St Andrew's Church, Bo'Ness reaches people through its website, www.theremustbemore.net on which it invites writers and ideas for a media team.

*Please send further examples to 'Church Models' on www.aidan.org.uk

A spiritual audit of a neighbourhood

1. Defining a neighbourhood

The range of definitions is as wide as is that for individuals. A person may be defined in purely physical terms, or in terms that include the moral and spiritual. The diagram below offers a hierarchy of criteria.

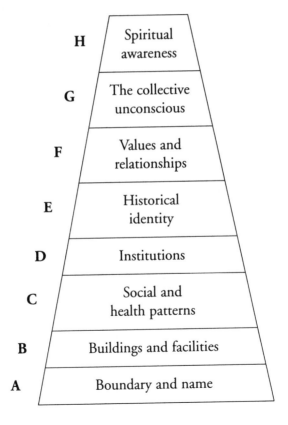

H — Spiritual awareness

G — The collective unconscious

F — Values and relationships

E — Historical identity

D — Institutions

C — Social and health patterns

B — Buildings and facilities

A — Boundary and name

2. A neighbourhood audit

Financial and efficiency audits were widely extended from business to the professions under Mrs Thatcher. Calls for social audits rightly increase. Most denominations have now introduced audits for churches.

Nowhere, as far as I know, has there been a spiritual audit of a neighbourhood. Swanley United Reformed Church, Kent, commissioned MARC Europe to do a survey of the community. It measured quantities (for example, of population and housing categories, facilities, crimes, diseases, house transfers, jobs, cars, births, deaths) but not qualities. There was little in the survey indicating whether, or to what degree, the neighbourhood was spiritually renewed.

Mission Audit Pack (Milton Keynes Christian Foundation, 4 Church Street, Wolverton, MK12 5JM) has some good suggestions.

An audit of the spirituality of a neighbourhood is more akin to an art than to a science. Its measurements must inevitably be more intuitive. Nevertheless, it has its own value.

A neighbourhood audit should map the eight areas in the pyramid.

A) Boundary and name

Spiritual renewal cannot come to a non-entity. The clearer the boundary (e.g. by river, earth mounds, greenbelts) the more chance there is of an identity.

- Mark the boundary of your parish/neighbourhood
- What is its population?
- How many feel this is where they belong (in answer to this question)?

- Is its name:
  - positive (e.g. Stoke Holy Cross)
  - neutral (e.g. Great Yarmouth)
  - negative (e.g. Dragonsthorpe)
- Revive the ancient Church of England custom of 'beating the bounds'.
- How many entrances and exits to the neighbourhood are there? Enclosure helps foster relationship.

B) Buildings and facilities

The criteria used by planners is economics – they may be based on selfish or spiritual values.

- List the public buildings and facilities
- Are the buildings standardised, or do they reflect a distinctive character?
- What needs are not met inside the neighbourhood?

C) Social and health patterns

Transport is a key to neighbourhood. Too much through traffic, or too high a percentage of two-car households can deaden community. If dominant social and health needs are met from outside the area, or if there is too high a percentage of depressed people in the area, community is negated.

- What is the housing mix?
- What percentage of the population is under 18, 18-60, over 60?
- How many households have access to a car?
- What is the population turnover each year?
- Simulate a day in the life of a single mother, an unemployed school leaver, and a house-bound pensioner.

- Which of these are available within the area: shops, schools, surgery/chemist, pub, leisure, religious centre?

D) Institutions

An area which has factors A-C may still be a mere collection of people with a consumer mentality. If it has institutions ('the lengthened shadow of one man', Emerson) it has the beginnings of true community.

- List the voluntary groups and activities in the neighbourhood.

E) Historical identity

Awareness of its story is necessary to neighbourhood. Roots matter. 'To exist is to have a place, a space that is recognised by others', Tournier. A small weak church decided to trace and tell its story to the neighbourhood. It revived. Boris Pasternak, who survived Stalin's purges, saw his mission as 'witnessing the tragedy, carrying it inside himself', to be fully expressed when the time finally came (Andrew Netursov, *The Times* 4 January 1990). The soul of a neighbourhood may depend upon even one person carrying its story not its meaning inside himself so it can be fully expressed when the right time comes.

- What visual reminders of your neighbourhood's history are there?

- What published reminders are there?

- What projects do the schools or church do on local history?

F) Values and relationships

The making of good connections between the groups and networks in a neighbourhood is essential to its spiritual renewal.

- Which of these agencies relate regularly with most or all of the others: Health, Social Services, Police, Church, Schools, Local Authority, Voluntary Workers?
- Which schools/young people's groups relate to old people's groups, sheltered housing, etc.?
- Which of the voluntary groups have church representatives?
- Is respect for old people, young people, Christian marriage, the church, property, the local environment, typical of over or under 50 per cent of the population, and of the local committees? What about positive welcome for the same?

G) The collective unconscious

C. J. Jung, in his study of the collective unconscious, stated that the deeper layers of the psyche lose their individual uniqueness and become 'increasingly collective' (*Collected Works*, para 29) He discovered psychic tracts were peculiar to specific cultures. The Bible refers to psychic spirits or binding spirits from the past. These seem to be referred to in Romans 8:38 and Ephesians 6:12; the Greek word 'archai' is sometimes translated as 'principalities'.

- What occult, hostile or hard influences are evident in the past history of the neighbourhood?
- What visible or spiritual signs of resistance are there?
- What are the signs of good?

H) Spiritual awareness

The spirit of a place is a constantly evolving cluster of qualities. Taken as a whole the dominant spirit may be that of pleasure, apathy, fear, friendships, greed or love of God.

- What percentage of the population are committed Christians?

- In answer to the question 'Where, if anywhere, is your spiritual home?', what percentage of the population would say its neighbourhood church?
- What percentage of the population use the church buildings or houses weekly for:
    worship
    quiet prayer
    groups
    fellowship
    creative/social activities?
- What percentage of the homes have daily prayer?
- What percentage of the homes have a Christian symbol?
- What percentage of the population have used the church building or staff in the last year?

These are just some suggestions for taking the spiritual temperature of a neighbourhood. You could suggest others.

APPENDIX 3

The church as a stool with three legs

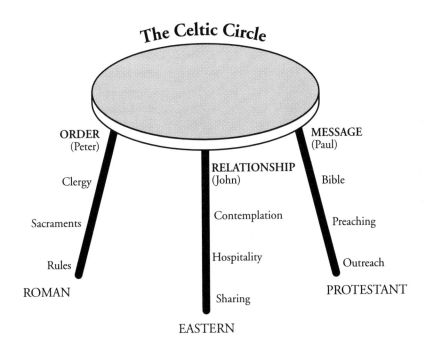

The Celtic Circle

ORDER
(Peter)

Clergy

Sacraments

Rules

ROMAN

RELATIONSHIP
(John)

Contemplation

Hospitality

Sharing

EASTERN

MESSAGE
(Paul)

Bible

Preaching

Outreach

PROTESTANT

APPENDIX 4

Networking the neighbourhood –
a process for neighbourhood church

The church in a neighbourhood is like a heart in a body. The heart cannot bring renewal to the body (the neighbourhood) if it is detached from the arteries (the neighbourhood network), or if the arteries are blocked.

The diagram illustrates this:

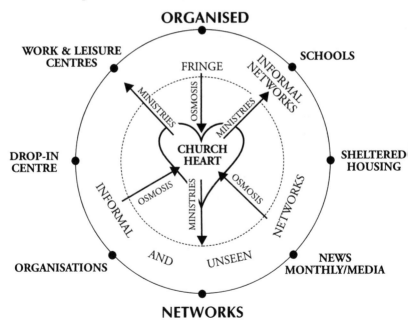

The heart

The heart represents the praise, faith, prayer, nurture, love, work, fellowship and celebration of the Christian community.

The priests at Medugorge try to create a spiritual environment that will sustain the movement of ongoing conversion in the parishioners. The various prayer groups, communities and seminars 'are like posts in a fence; without the posts the fence collapses'. Those in the groups go more deeply into the movement of conversion (*Medugorge Unfolds*, Fowler Wright).

If the heart is to transform the neighbourhood, church members need a right attitude towards neighbours:

- The main sphere of service is the residents
- 'He who is not against me is for me' (Jesus)
- We should be united with our neighbour in everything except sin
- We should aim to be secure enough in God to share human things in common with our neighbours
- Christian jargon and outdated language, which alienates non-Christians, should not be used.

If the heart is to transform the neighbourhood, the church needs an appropriate agenda for the neighbourhool.

Most residents (especially in urban areas) perceive the church as a privatised concern for the minority who want religion. They do not feel the church is in solidarity with their good but non-religious aspirations. Raymond Fung, Evangelism Secretary of the World Council of Churches, urges each church to draw up an agenda with people of goodwill in the neighbourhood. He calls this an Isaiah agenda, because passages such as Isaiah 65:20-23 provide examples of agendas of fairness and peace, which require partnership with the world. (*How a Local Congregation Evangelises and Grows*, C.W.M.C., W.C.C. 150 Rte de Ferney, B.P. 21000, 1211 Geneva, 0053c/12-13, Switzerland). A dynamic equivalent of Isaiah's agenda could be:

• Every child cherished from conception
• Every old person living a full life and dying in dignity
• Every person having a place where they belong
• Every person finding creative work and enjoying its fruits
• Joy and safety in the streets
• Young and old in harmony with each other, the environment and God.

Church ministries – the outward arrows

These represent church ministries that reach people on the fringe of the church life. The Engel Scale suggests that the population is made up of people with various levels of awareness of God. The majority of conversions come from people who do not only believe in a supernatural being, but who also have some relationship with the church. Therefore a strategy to enlarge the church fringe makes sense.

This could include ministries to families, children, mothers, men, the bereaved, pastoral, healing, counselling, evangelistic or special events ministries.

Examples:

• house-to-house visiting ministries
• inviting them to fill up prayer request cards, survey forms, etc.
• to receive Gospels, prayer cards, crosses
• to have annual house blessings
• to subscribe to Bible notes
• to come to special events at the church centre or to a 'down your street' party.

Osmosis – the inward arrows

Osmosis is a biological process which echoes the process of human friendship. As local Christians draw in human life from friends they make in the natural course of events (neighbours, shopping, schools, groups, pubs, sports, etc.), so their friends in turn imbibe their life, which includes Christ. Christ in the believer filters out impurities that would otherwise be imbibed from their friendships: the filters make rejection of these people unnecessary. Friendship has proved to be the most effective form of evangelism.

Informal and unseen networks – the broken lines

The informal networks of communication include the spontaneous gatherings at funerals, christenings, weddings and anniversaries; gatherings at the school gates, launderette, clinic, chemist, playgroup; tupperware type parties; special events (at Christmas, fireworks night, Remembrance, for example). They include wardens of special housing centres, caretakers of large buildings, ringleaders of young people, gathering points, such as bus shelters, parks or car parks, and matriarchs who know everyone in their street!

The unseen networks include historical memories, psychic or spiritual vibrations which may focus around ancient, quiet or religious places, ley lines, groves or buildings with occult or psychic auras, video shops.

Organised networks – the outer circle

These may include schools and educational services; the voluntary organisations, sports and leisure activities, local news magazines; statutory agencies such as police, doctors, social workers, housing officers; local councillors; the parish council or residents' associations; old people's homes, agencies; shops, centres and employment units.

The church and the neighbourhood network

It is clear that if the church is to use the neighbourgood networks effectively it needs not only a right attitude, and a neighbourhood agenda that speaks to residents' aspirations, but also a practical programme for each network.

The value of the unseen army of intercessors and contemplatives for the unconscious network cannot be over estimated. A church meeting or weekend away could discover who is involved in each of the informal channels of communication, and pray for people to fill the gaps.

The formal network needs an organised approach. For example, staff or volunteers who visit every voluntary organisation to affirm what is worthwhile in their work. Sometimes agencies compete or specialise so that the individual feels no one is concerned for her or him as a whole person. The church can play the role of co-ordinator between agencies, and seek to affirm that which is of God in each. Wherever possible, the church should publish or contribute to a local news magazine, and have notices in as many shops, centres and complexes as possible.

Things to do:

- Use a church council or church meeting to present a profile of 'Our attitude to our neighbours'.
- Fix an occasion to begin to draw up a neighbourhood agenda.
- Make a list of all informal foci of communication, and make another list of church members involved in each of them.
- Make a list of every organisation, centre and agency in the neighbourhood, and make another list of church members involved in each of them.

APPENDIX 5

Recommended further reading

Being Human: Being Church by Robert Warren (Marshall Pickering). Challenges churches to turn into missionary congregations and laboratories for becoming more fully human beings.

Changing World: Changing Church by Michael Monagh (Monarch Books 2001). A vital, well-researched, practically illustrated guide to how the church can be transformed.

Church Next by Eddie Gibbs (Covenant Publications).

Colonies of Heaven: Celtic Christian Communities by Ian Bradley (Darton, Longman & Todd, 2000). An insight into Celtic monastic people's churches and lessons for the church today.

Dying Church: Living God! A Call to Begin Again by Chuck Meyer (Northstone Publishing Canada) A barnstorming hit list!

Natural Church Development Book by Christian A. Schwarz (British Church Growth Association).

New Springtime of the Church by Christopher Donaldson (Canterbury Press) proposes a reshaping of the Church of England that reflects insights of Martin of Tours.

New Tasks for a Renewed Church by Tom Wright (Hodder & Stoughton 1992) urges churches to find focal points of the emerging new paganism, and ways of honouring Jesus as Lord within these. He calls for Christian 'shrines' to be established in various areas by: coming alongside those in pain as a result of war; proclaiming in liturgy and deeds that the powers of Mammon shall be brought low; celebrating sexuality; cherishing the earth; developing forgiving and respectful friendships with people of other faiths within which witness becomes authentic; restoring a sacramental approach to church life; rescuing from eastern monopoly the mystical and contemplative traditions of prayer; and restoring holism to intellectual endeavour.

New Way of Being Church – this series of booklets can be obtained from Pauline Lamming, Lodge Farm House, Groton, Sudbury, Suffolk CO10 5EJ.

Threshold of the Future: Reforming the Church in the Post-Christian West by Michael Riddell (SPCK 1998). This gives examples of churches in his native New Zealand which are pioneering new ways of being church, from 'Parallel Universe' to 'Spine'.

This Study Guide is one of a growing range of resources from the Community of Aidan and Hilda and is part of a movement to resource the emerging Church.

To keep in touch with this log on to:
www.aidan.org.uk

Sources and Acknowledgements

The author and publishers are grateful to the following for permission to reproduce their copyright material:

Wm. B. Eerdmans Publishing Co., Grand Rapids, MI, USA, for the Eugene H. Peterson quote from 'In the Belly of the Fish', a chapter in *Under the Unpredictable Plant*, © 1992, Eugene Peterson.

Excerpt from 'The Twenty-First Century Church' by Rick Joyner, September 1999, an article in *Prophetic Bulletin*, Copyright © Morning-Star Publications, Inc. Excerpts used by permission. To read the entire article, please visit www.MorningStarMinistries.org

Excerpt from *Out of Chaos: Refounding Religious Congregations* by Gerald A. Arbuckle, S.M., Copyright © 1988 by Gerald A. Arbuckle, Paulist Press, Inc., New York/Mahwah, N.J. Used with permission. www.paulistpress.com

Excerpt from *The Maternal Face of God: The Feminine and Its Religious Expressions* by Leonardo Boff, translated by Robert Barr and John Diecksmeier. Copyright © 1979 Leonardo Boff, and published in 1987 by Harper & Row, San Francisco, and in 1989 by Collins, UK.

Bishop Jim Thomson, Diocese of Bath and Wells, for kind permission to reproduce his quote on page 39. Copyright © Bishop Jim Thomson.

Clive Price, for kind permission to reproduce his quote on page 174. Copyright © Clive Price.

Every effort has been made to trace the owners of copyright material and it is hoped that no copyright has been infringed. Pardon is sought and apology made if the contrary be the case and a correction will be made in any reprint of this book.